PRIMARY MATHEMATICS Standards Edition

TEXTBOOK

Marshall Cavendish
Education

SM Singapore Math Inc®

Blank

Original edition published under the title Primary Mathematics Textbook 4B
© 1983 Curriculum Planning & Development Division, Ministry of Education, Singapore
Published by Times Media Private Limited

This edition © 2008 Marshall Cavendish International (Singapore) Private Limited
© 2014 Marshall Cavendish Education Pte Ltd
(Formerly known as Marshall Cavendish International (Singapore) Private Limited)

Published by Marshall Cavendish Education
Times Centre, 1 New Industrial Road, Singapore 536196
Customer Service Hotline: (65) 6213 9444
US Office Tel: (1-914) 332 8888 I Fax: (1-914) 332 8882
E-mail: tmesales@mceducation.com
Website: www.mceducation.com

Marshall Cavendish Corporation
99 White Plains Road
Tarrytown, NY 10591
U.S.A.
Tel: (1-914) 332 8888
Fax: (1-914) 332 8882
E-mail: mcc@marshallcavendish.com
Website: www.marshallcavendish.com

Singapore Math Inc®
Distributed by
Singapore Math Inc.®
19535 SW 129th Avenue
Tualatin, OR 97062
U.S.A.
Website: www.singaporemath.com

First published 2008
Reprinted 2009 (twice), 2010, 2011, 2012 (twice), 2014, 2015

Primary Mathematics (Standards Edition) Textbook 4B
ISBN 978-0-7614-6984-1

Printed in Malaysia

Primary Mathematics (Standards Edition) is adapted from Primary Mathematics Textbook 4B (3rd Edition), originally developed by the Ministry of Education, Singapore. This edition contains new content developed by Marshall Cavendish International (Singapore) Private Limited, which is not attributable to the Ministry of Education, Singapore.

We would like to acknowledge the Project Team from the Ministry of Education, Singapore, that developed the original Singapore Edition:
Project Director: Dr Kho Tek Hong
Team Members: Hector Chee Kum Hoong, Chip Wai Lung, Liang Hin Hoon, Lim Eng Tann,
                Rosalind Lim Hui Cheng, Ng Hwee Wan, Ng Siew Lee
Curriculum Specialists: Christina Cheong Ngan Peng, Ho Juan Beng

Our thanks to Richard Askey, Emeritus Professor of Mathematics (University of Wisconsin, Madison) and Madge Goldman, President (Gabriella and Paul Rosenbaum Foundation), for their help and advice in the production of Primary Mathematics (Standards Edition).

We would also like to recognize the contributions of Jennifer Kempe (Curriculum Advisor, Singapore Math Inc.®) and Bill Jackson (Math Coach, School No. 2, Paterson, New Jersey) to Primary Mathematics (Standards Edition).

Mathematics Content Standards for California Public Schools reproduced by permission, California Department of Education, CDE Press, 1430 N Street, Suite 3207, Sacramento, CA 95814.

PREFACE

PRIMARY MATHEMATICS (Standards Edition) is a complete program from the publishers of Singapore's successful *Primary Mathematics* series. Newly adapted to align with the Mathematics Framework for California Public Schools, the program aims to equip students with sound concept development, critical thinking and efficient problem-solving skills.

Mathematical concepts are introduced in the opening pages and taught to mastery through specific learning tasks that allow for immediate assessment and consolidation.

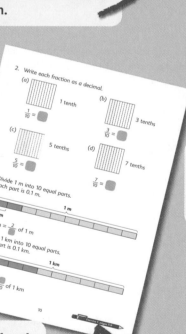

The **modeling method** enables students to visualize and solve mathematical problems quickly and efficiently.

The **Concrete → Pictorial → Abstract** approach enables students to encounter math in a meaningful way and translate mathematical skills from the concrete to the abstract.

The **pencil icon** ✏️ Exercise 18, pages 18-20 provides quick and easy reference from the Textbook to the relevant Workbook pages. The **direct correlation** of the Workbook to the Textbook facilitates focused review and evaluation.

New mathematical concepts are introduced through a **spiral progression** that builds on concepts already taught and mastered.

Metacognition is employed as a strategy for learners to monitor their thinking processes in problem solving. Speech and thought bubbles provide guidance through the thought processes, making even the most challenging problems accessible to students.

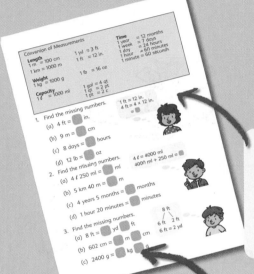

The color patch ▮ is used to invite active student participation and to facilitate lively discussion about the mathematical concepts taught.

Regular **reviews** in the Textbook provide consolidation of concepts learned.

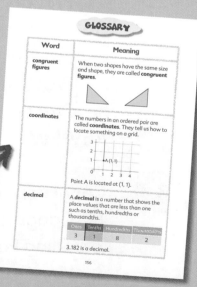

The **glossary** effectively combines pictorial representation with simple mathematical definitions to provide a comprehensive reference guide for students.

CONTENTS

6 DECIMALS

1 Tenths

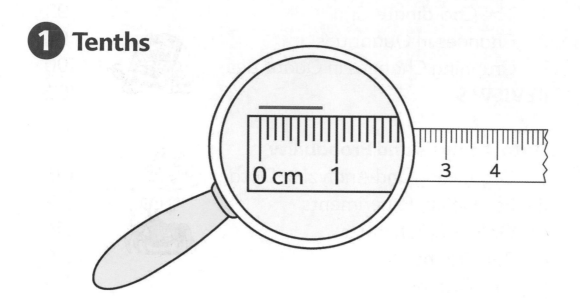

The length of the string is $\frac{8}{10}$ cm or 0.8 cm.

$0.8 = \frac{8}{10}$

We read 0.8 as **zero point eight** or as **eight tenths**.

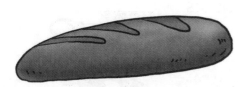

The weight of the bread is 0.8 kg.

The amount of water is 0.8 ℓ.

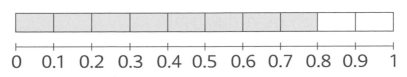

0 0.1 0.2 0.3 0.4 0.5 0.6 0.7 0.8 0.9 1

0.8 is 8 tenths.

Numbers like 0.1 and 0.8 are **decimals**.
The dot '.' in a decimal is called a **decimal point**.

> Divide 1 whole into 10 equal parts. Each part is $\frac{1}{10}$ or 0.1.

1.

1 one   10 tenths

Write a decimal for each of the following.

(a)

4 tenths = ▢

(b)

0.1 0.1 0.1 0.1 0.1 0.1

6 tenths = ▢

(c)

0.1 0.1 0.1 0.1 0.1
0.1 0.1 0.1 0.1

9 tenths = ▢

2. Write each fraction as a decimal.

(a)

1 tenth

$$\frac{1}{10} = \text{⬛}$$

(b)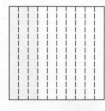

3 tenths

$$\frac{3}{10} = \text{⬛}$$

(c)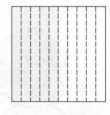

5 tenths

$$\frac{5}{10} = \text{⬛}$$

(d)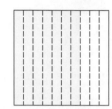

7 tenths

$$\frac{7}{10} = \text{⬛}$$

3. Divide 1 m into 10 equal parts.
Each part is 0.1 m.

1 m

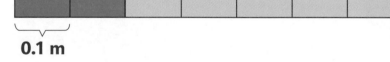

0.1 m

$$0.2 \text{ m} = \frac{2}{\text{⬛}} \text{ of 1 m}$$

4. Divide 1 km into 10 equal parts.
Each part is 0.1 km.

1 km

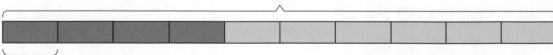

0.1 km

$$0.4 \text{ km} = \frac{\text{⬛}}{10} \text{ of 1 km}$$

Exercise 1, pages 7-9

5.

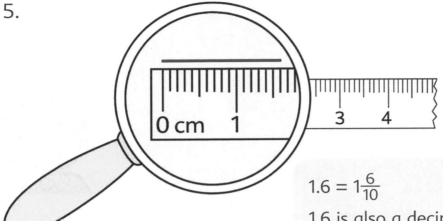

$$1.6 = 1\frac{6}{10}$$

1.6 is also a decimal.
We read 1.6 as **one point six**
or as **one and six tenths**.

The length of the string is 1.6 cm.

(a) 1.6 cm is [ ] cm longer than 1 cm.

(b) 1.6 = 1 + [ ]

6. (a)

The total amount of water is [ ] ℓ.

(b)

The total weight of the butter is [ ] kg.

Exercise 2, pages 10-11

7. Write each fraction as a decimal.

   (a) 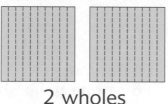 $1\frac{5}{10} =$ 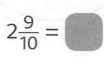 $1\frac{5}{10} = 1 + \frac{5}{10}$

   1 whole 5 tenths

   (b) 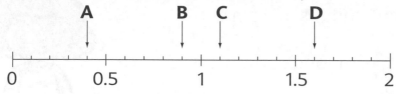 $2\frac{9}{10} =$ ☐

   2 wholes   9 tenths

8. Write the decimal represented by each letter.

   A   B   C   D

   |———|———|———|———|———|———|———|———|
   0   0.5   1   1.5   2

9. Write each decimal as a fraction in its simplest form.

   (a) $0.2 = \frac{2}{10}$ (b) $1.2 = 1\frac{2}{10}$

       $=$ ☐ $=$ ☐ $1.2 = 1 + 0.2$

   (c) $0.8 =$ ☐   (d) $2.8 =$ ☐

10. Which number is the smallest?

    6.4,   5.8,   3.7,   9.1

11. Which number is the greatest?

    2.7,   4.8,   8.5,   1.6

12. Arrange the numbers in increasing order.
    (a) 3.1,   0.3,   3,   1.3

    (b) 7.2,   2.7,   9,   7.8

13. Complete the following regular number patterns.

(a) 6.0, 6.2, 6.4, 6.6 ▢ , ▢

(b) 8.0, 8.4, 8.8, ▢ , ▢ , 10

Exercise 3, pages 12-13

14. Write a decimal for each of the following.

(a) ① ①   0.1 0.1 0.1 $2 + 0.3 = $ ▢

2 ones   3 tenths

(b) 10 10   1 1   0.1 0.1
   10   1 1   0.1 0.1
     1 1   0.1 $30 + 6 + 0.5 = $ ▢

3 tens   6 ones   5 tenths

(c) 10 10   0.1 0.1
  10 10   0.1 0.1
   10

5 tens   4 tenths $50 + 0.4 = $ ▢

15. Write a decimal for each of the following.

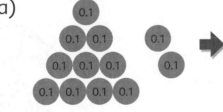

(a)

12 tenths = ▢

12 tenths = 1 one 2 tenths

(b)

21 tenths = ▢

Exercise 4, pages 14-15

② Hundredths

What is the length of the colored part?

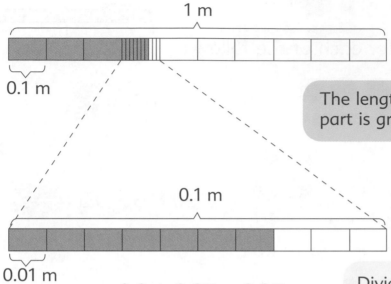

1 m

0.1 m

The length of the colored part is greater than 0.3 m.

0.1 m

0.01 m

$$0.3 + 0.07 = 0.37$$

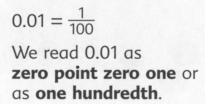
Divide 0.1 m into 10 equal parts. Each part is 0.01 m.

The length of the colored part is 0.37 m.

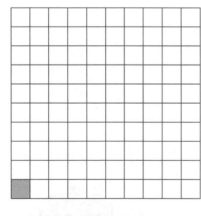

0.01 is 1 hundredth.

$0.01 = \frac{1}{100}$

We read 0.01 as **zero point zero one** or as **one hundredth**.

0.07 is 7 hundredths.

$0.07 = \frac{7}{100}$

We read 0.07 as **zero point zero seven** or as **seven hundredths**.

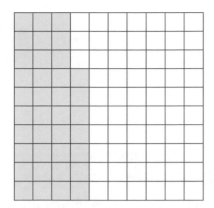

0.37 is 37 hundredths.

$0.37 = \frac{37}{100}$

We read 0.37 as **zero point three seven** or as **thirty-seven hundredths**.

0.37 is 3 tenths 7 hundredths.

$$0.37 = \frac{3}{10} + \frac{7}{100}$$

1.

1 tenth   10 hundredths

Write a decimal for each of the following.

(a)

3 hundredths =

(b)

5 hundredths =

(c)

12 hundredths =

2. Write a decimal for each of the following.

(a)

3 ones   2 hundredths

$3 + 0.02 = 3.02$

We read 3.02 as **three point zero two** or as **three and two hundredths**.

(b)

| 1 | 1 | | 0.1 | 0.1 | | 0.01 | 0.01 | 0.01 |
| 1 | 1 | | | | | 0.01 | 0.01 | |

$4 + 0.2 + 0.05 = $

4 ones   2 tenths   5 hundredths

3.

Hundreds	Tens	Ones	Tenths	Hundredths
100	10	1 1	0.1 0.1	0.01 0.01 0.01
100	10 10	1 1	0.1 0.1 0.1	0.01 0.01 0.01

In 234.56, the digit 2 stands for 200.
What does each of the other digits stand for?

4.

Hundreds	Tens	Ones	Tenths	Hundredths
3	4	7	9	2

The number 347.92 has two decimal places.

The digit 9 is in the tenths place. Its value is .

The digit 2 is in the hundredths place. Its value is .

What is the value of each of the other digits?

The tenths place and the hundredths place are called **decimal places**.

Exercise 5, pages 16-18

5. Write each fraction as a decimal.

(a)

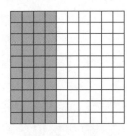

40 hundredths

$\frac{40}{100} = \frac{4}{10}$

$\frac{40}{100} = $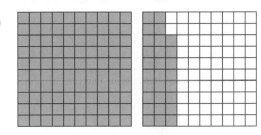

(b)

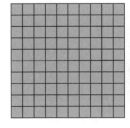

1 whole 28 hundredths

$1\frac{28}{100} = $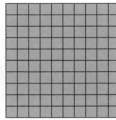

(c)

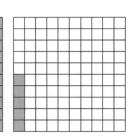

2 wholes
5 hundredths

$2\frac{5}{100} = $

6.

(a) $0.01 = 1¢

$0.01 is $\dfrac{\boxed{}}{100}$ of $1.

(b) $0.10 = 10¢

$0.10 is $\dfrac{\boxed{}}{10}$ of $1.

(c) $0.20 is $\dfrac{\boxed{}}{10}$ of $1.

$0.20 = $\boxed{}$ ¢

(d) 50¢ is $\dfrac{\boxed{}}{10}$ of $1.

50¢ = $\boxed{}$

(e) $0.45 is $\dfrac{\boxed{}}{100}$ of $1.

$0.45 = $\boxed{}$ ¢

(f) 26¢ is $\dfrac{\boxed{}}{100}$ of $1.

26¢ = $\boxed{}$

7. Write each of the following amounts of money as a decimal.
    (a) 3 dollars 85 cents   (b) 6 dollars 50 cents
    (c) 8 dollars 5 cents   (d) 85 dollars

Exercise 6, pages 19-20

8. Write a decimal for each of the following.
    (a) 2 + 0.84   (b) 30 + 6 + 0.25
    (c) 54 + 0.03   (d) 80 + 0.5 + 0.07

9. Complete the following regular number patterns.

(a) 3, 3.3, 3.6 [ ], [ ], 4.5

(b) 9, 8.8, 8.6, [ ], [ ], 8

(c) 4.65, 4.7, [ ], 4.8, [ ], 4.9

10. What decimal does each letter represent?

(a)

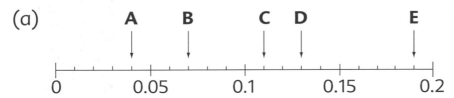

(b)

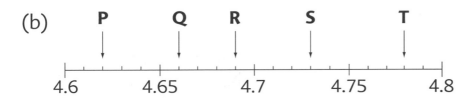

Exercise 7, pages 21-22

11. (a) Express 0.25 as a fraction in its simplest form.

$$0.25 = \frac{25}{100}$$

$$= \boxed{}$$

(b) Express 1.84 as a fraction in its simplest form.

$$1.84 = 1\frac{84}{100}$$

$$= \boxed{}$$

12. Express each decimal as a fraction in its simplest form.

    (a) 0.06   (b) 0.28   (c) 0.24

    (d) 2.05   (e) 3.65   (f) 4.75

13. (a) Express $\frac{3}{5}$ as a decimal.

$$\frac{3}{5} = \frac{\boxed{}}{10}$$

$$= \boxed{}$$

$\frac{3}{5}$ can be changed into a fraction which has a denominator of 10.

    (b) Express $\frac{9}{20}$ as a decimal.

$$\frac{9}{20} = \frac{\boxed{}}{100}$$

$$= \boxed{}$$

$\frac{9}{20}$ can be changed into a fraction which has a denominator of 100.

14. Express each fraction as a decimal.

    (a) $\frac{3}{4}$ (b) $\frac{7}{20}$ (c) $\frac{8}{25}$

    (d) $1\frac{1}{2}$ (e) $2\frac{2}{5}$ (f) $3\frac{27}{50}$

Exercise 8, pages 23-24

15. Write > or < in place of each .

(a)

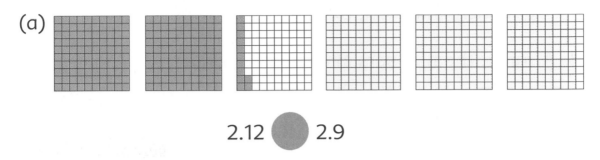

2.12 2.9

(b)

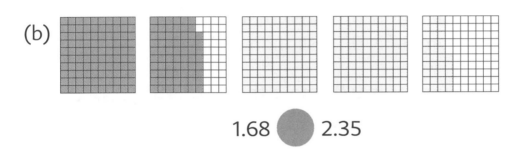

1.68 2.35

16. (a) Which is greater, 562.41 or 562.38?

Hundreds	Tens	Ones	Tenths	Hundredths
5	6	2	**4**	1
5	6	2	**3**	8

(b) Which is smaller, 89.67 or 243.5?

Hundreds	Tens	Ones	Tenths	Hundredths
	8	9	6	7
2	4	3	5	

17. (a) Which is greater, 42.6 or 42.06?
    (b) Which is longer, 2.38 m or 2.5 m?
    (c) Which is heavier, 32.6 kg or 3.26 kg?

18. Arrange the numbers in decreasing order.

    (a) 2.02,   0.2,   0.02,   2.2
    (b) 74.5,   7.45,   7.8,   80.7

 Exercise 9, pages 25-26

19. (a) What number is 0.1 more than 412.34?
    (b) What number is 0.1 less than 412.34?

20. (a) What number is 0.01 more than 123.48?
    (b) What number is 0.01 less than 123.48?

21. (a) Add 3 tenths to 4.87. The answer is .

    (b) Subtract 2 hundredths from 28.62. The answer is .

22. Find the value of each of the following.

    (a) 86.43 + 0.2   (b) 24.8 + 0.05   (c) 4.87 + 0.02
    (d) 54.62 − 0.4   (e) 6.23 − 0.03   (f) 3.48 − 0.05

23. (a) 36.54 is   more than 36.

    (b) 36.54 is   more than 36.5.

24. What number must be added to 0.82   82 + 18 = 100
    to give the answer 1?

Exercise 10, pages 27-28

③ Thousandths

> 1 hundredth = 10 thousandths
> We read 0.001 as **zero point zero zero one** or as **one thousandth**.

Write a decimal for each of the following.

(a)

2 hundredths 4 thousandths =

(b)

3 tenths 1 hundredth 5 thousandths =

(c)

4 ones 2 thousandths =

1.

Tens	Ones		Tenths	Hundredths	Thousandths
10 10			0.1 0.1 0.1 0.1	0.01 0.01 0.01	0.001 0.001 0.001 0.001 0.001

20.435 has 3 decimal places.

(a) The digit 5 is in the thousandths place. What is its value?

(b) What is the value of each of the other digits?

> We read 20.435 as **twenty point four three five** or as **twenty and four hundred thirty-five thousandths**.

2. (a) What number is 0.01 more than 5.62?
   (b) What number is 0.01 less than 5.62?
   (c) What number is 0.001 more than 4.536?
   (d) What number is 0.001 less than 4.536?

3. What is the missing number in each ⬜?

   (a) 27.148 is ⬜ more than 27.

   (b) 27.148 is ⬜ more than 27.1.

   (c) 27.148 is ⬜ more than 27.14.

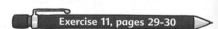
Exercise 11, pages 29-30

4. (a) Which is greater, 42.54 or 42.326?

Tens	Ones	Tenths	Hundredths	Thousandths
4	2	**5**	4	0
4	2	**3**	2	6

(b) Which is smaller, 63.182 or 63.187?

Tens	Ones	Tenths	Hundredths	Thousandths
6	3	1	8	**2**
6	3	1	8	**7**

5. Arrange the numbers in decreasing order.

   (a) 0.32,   0.302,   0.032,   3.02
   (b) 2.139,   2.628,   2.045,   2.189

6. Arrange the numbers in increasing order.

   (a) 5.8,   0.538,   0.83,   3.58
   (b) 9.047,   9.076,   9.074,   9.067

Exercise 12, page 31

7. Express 0.052 as a fraction in its simplest form.

   $0.052 = \dfrac{52}{1000}$

   $=$ ⬜

8. Express each decimal as a fraction in its simplest form.

   (a) 0.5
   (b) 0.08
   (c) 0.024
   (d) 0.345

9. Express 2.045 as a fraction in its simplest form.

   $2.045 = 2\dfrac{45}{1000}$

   $=$ ⬜

10. Express each decimal as a fraction in its simplest form.

    (a) 2.6
    (b) 6.05
    (c) 3.002
    (d) 2.408

11. Arrange the numbers in increasing order.

    (a) $\dfrac{4}{5}$,   0.652,   2,   0.6

    (b) 7.231, $\dfrac{7}{25}$, $1\dfrac{3}{4}$,   0.35

Exercise 13, pages 32-33

PRACTICE A

1. What is the value of the digit 6 in each of the following?

   (a) 1.**6**58   (b) **6**.185   (c) 3.0**6**9   (d) 5.74**6**

2. What is the missing number in each ?

   (a) In 3.864, the digit ▢ is in the thousandths place.

   (b) In 49.73, the digit ▢ is in the tenths place.

3. (a) What number is 0.1 less than 5.609?
   (b) What number is 0.01 more than 2.809?
   (c) What number is 0.001 less than 13.521?

4. Find the value of each of the following.

   (a) 0.7 + 0.02   (b) 3.7 + 0.08

   (c) 5.82 − 0.02   (d) 8.94 − 0.9

5. Express each decimal as a fraction in its simplest form.

   (a) 0.08   (b) 0.14   (c) 0.145   (d) 0.408
   (e) 3.6   (f) 1.12   (g) 4.506   (h) 2.006

6. Express each fraction as a decimal.

   (a) $\dfrac{9}{10}$ (b) $\dfrac{3}{100}$ (c) $\dfrac{39}{1000}$ (d) $\dfrac{105}{1000}$

   (e) $1\dfrac{7}{10}$ (f) $2\dfrac{18}{100}$ (g) $3\dfrac{7}{1000}$ (h) $\dfrac{999}{1000}$

7. What is the missing number in each ?

   (a) $8.07 = 8 +$ ▢   (b) $6.805 = 6 + 0.8 +$ ▢

   (c) $5.012 = 5 + \dfrac{1}{100} + \dfrac{▢}{1000}$ (d) $2.004 = 2 + \dfrac{4}{▢}$

PRACTICE B

1. Arrange the numbers in increasing order.

   (a) 0.008, 0.09, 0.08, 0.009
   (b) 3.25, 3.205, 3.025, 3.502
   (c) 4.386, 4.683, 4.638, 4.9
   (d) 10, 9.932, 9.392, 9.923

2. Express each fraction as a decimal.

   (a) $\frac{1}{2}$ (b) $\frac{3}{4}$ (c) $\frac{1}{5}$

   (d) $\frac{19}{5}$ (e) $6\frac{1}{4}$ (f) $4\frac{3}{5}$

3. Replace each ⬤ with >, <, or =.

   (a) $\frac{47}{1000}$ ⬤ 0.047   (b) 0.205 ⬤ $\frac{25}{1000}$

   (c) $3\frac{3}{5}$ ⬤ 3.69   (d) 2.8 ⬤ $2\frac{4}{5}$

   (e) 1.425 ⬤ $1\frac{1}{4}$ (f) 0.87 ⬤ $\frac{78}{100}$

4. Write each of the following as a decimal.

   (a) $1 + \frac{7}{10} + \frac{3}{1000}$ (b) $\frac{8}{100} + \frac{5}{1000}$

   (c) $5 + \frac{6}{100} + \frac{9}{1000}$ (d) $10 + \frac{52}{1000}$

5. Write a decimal for each of the following.

   (a) 0.2 + 0.04 + 0.008   (b) 0.7 + 0.09 + 0.002
   (c) 3 + 0.7 + 0.08   (d) 10 + 0.5 + 0.004
   (e) 7 + 0.009   (f) 9 + 0.8 + 0.003

4 Rounding

The height of this hill is 164.3 m.

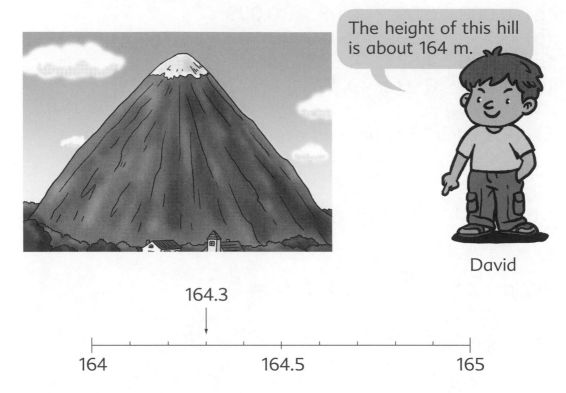

> The height of this hill is about 164 m.

David

164.3

164   164.5   165

David rounds 164.3 to the nearest whole number.

> 164.3 is between 164 and 165. It is nearer to 164 than to 165.

David

164.3 is 164 when rounded to the nearest whole number.

1. John weighs 37.4 kg.
   Round his weight to the nearest kilogram.

   37.4

   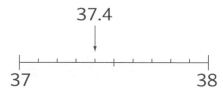

   37

   38

   37.4 is less than halfway between 37 and 38. It is rounded to 37.

   John's weight is ⬜ kg when rounded to the nearest kilogram.

2. A tree is 5.78 m tall.
   Round its height to the nearest meter.

   5.78 is more than halfway between 5 and 6. It is rounded to 6.

   5.78

   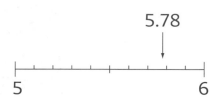

   5

   6

   The height of the tree is ⬜ m when rounded to the nearest meter.

3. Round 24.5 to the nearest whole number.

   24.5

   24

   25

   24.5 is halfway between 24 and 25. We take 25 to be the nearest whole number.

   24.5 is ⬜ when rounded to the nearest whole number.

4. Round each of the following to the nearest whole number.

    (a) 4.2   (b) 13.9   (c) 29.5

    (d) 5.45   (e) 15.64   (f) 18.52

Exercise 14, pages 34-35

5. The length of a string is 3.18 m.
    (a) Round 3.18 m to the nearest meter.

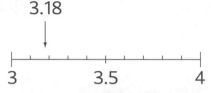

3.18 is smaller than 3.5.

    3.18 m is ⬜ m when rounded to the nearest meter.

    (b) Round 3.18 m to 1 decimal place.

3.18 is greater than 3.15.

    3.18 m is ⬜ m when rounded to 1 decimal place.

6.

                4.26   4.32 4.35

    4.2   4.3   4.4

    (a) 4.26 is ⬜ when rounded to 1 decimal place.

    (b) 4.32 is ⬜ when rounded to 1 decimal place.

    (c) 4.35 is ⬜ when rounded to 1 decimal place.

7. Round each of the following to 1 decimal place.

    (a) 0.91   (b) 2.45   (c) 7.08
    (d) 10.96   (e) 18.01   (f) 24.55

Exercise 15, page 36

REVIEW 6

1. What is the missing number in each 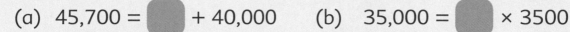?

   (a) $45,700 = \boxed{} + 40,000$ (b) $35,000 = \boxed{} \times 3500$

   (c) $91,548 = \boxed{} + 1548$ (d) $67,320 = 67,000 + \boxed{}$

2. Write the missing number in each 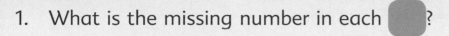.

   (a) $57.42 = 57 + \boxed{} + 0.02$ (b) $9.62 = 9.6 + \boxed{}$

   (c) $2.53 = 2 + \dfrac{5}{10} + \dfrac{\boxed{}}{100}$ (d) $26.48 = 26 + \dfrac{48}{\boxed{}}$

3. Arrange the numbers in decreasing order.

   (a) 3.03,   0.3,   0.03,   3.3
   (b) 0.05,   0.29,   0.305,   0.009

4. Find the value of each of the following.

   (a) $30 + 0.06$ (b) $73.26 - 0.06$

5. Round each of the following to the nearest whole number.

   (a) 3.2   (b) 10.09   (c) 4.55   (d) 19.51

6. Round each of the following to 1 decimal place.

   (a) 0.82   (b) 0.09   (c) 2.65   (d) 20.55

7. Round each of the following to the nearest ten.

   (a) 589   (b) 2834   (c) 12,097

8. Round each of the following to the nearest hundred.

   (a) 5650   (b) 13,845   (c) 45,090

9. (a) What number is 0.05 less than 4.1?
    (b) What number is 0.05 more than 4.1?
    (c) What number is 5 less than 0?
    (d) What number is 5 more than −10?

10. The sum of two numbers is 40. If one number is 3 times as big as the other number, find the difference between the two numbers.

11. Write down the common factors of 14 and 35.

12. Write down the first two common multiples of 4 and 6.

13. Write down the first prime number greater than 20.

14. What are the prime numbers between 10 and 15?

15. (a) Find the product of 13 and 469.
    (b) Find the quotient and remainder when 3278 is divided by 9.

16. What is the greatest whole number that can be placed in each ▢?

    (a) 5 + ▢ < 50   (b) 5 × ▢ < 50

17. Write >, <, or = in place of each ⬤.
    (a) −20 ⬤ −40
    (b) 15,060 ⬤ 1506 × 10
    (c) 4,567,200 ⬤ 5,567,200 − 1,000,000
    (d) 24 + 12 × 5 ⬤ (24 + 12) × 5
    (e) 5 × 4 × 6 ⬤ 3 × 8 × 4

18. $\frac{2}{2}$ $\frac{5}{8}$ $\frac{5}{12}$ $2\frac{9}{10}$ $1\frac{1}{9}$ $1\frac{11}{12}$

   (a) Which of the numbers is nearest to 2?

   (b) Which one of them is smaller than $\frac{1}{2}$?

19. Add or subtract. Give each answer in its simplest form.

   (a) $\frac{2}{3}+\frac{4}{9}$ (b) $\frac{5}{8}+\frac{3}{4}$ (c) $4-\frac{7}{10}$ (d) $6-\frac{3}{4}$

20. Find the value of each of the following.

   (a) $\frac{3}{5}$ of 15   (b) $\frac{2}{3}$ of 600   (c) $\frac{4}{9}$ of 99

21. Express each of the following as a decimal.

   (a) $4\frac{3}{100}$ (b) $1\frac{3}{5}$ (c) $10\frac{17}{20}$ (d) $5\frac{3}{4}$

22. Express each of the following as a fraction in its simplest form.

   (a) 0.8   (b) 1.25   (c) 4.45   (d) 6.06

23. Write a decimal in each ▢.

   (a)
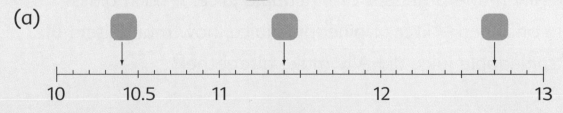

   (b)
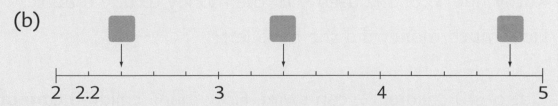

33

24. What fraction of each figure is shaded?
    Write the fractions in their simplest form.

    (a) 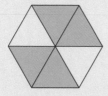   (b)

25. What type of quadrilateral is formed by the
    overlap when two sheets of paper are placed
    on top of each other as shown?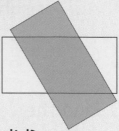

26. Which one of the following can be a net of a solid?

 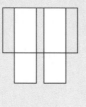 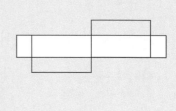

    A   **B**   **C**   **D**

27. There are 215 pens and 5 times as many pencils in a box.
    (a) How many more pencils than pens are there?
    (b) What is the total number of pens and pencils?

28. Ally made 5 glasses of pineapple juice. If each glass
    contained $\frac{2}{5}$ liter of pineapple juice, how many liters of
    pineapple juice did Ally make altogether?

29. Kathy had $20. She used $\frac{3}{4}$ of the money to buy a book.
    How much money did she have left?

30. Out of 40 children, $\frac{4}{5}$ can swim. How many children **cannot**
    swim?

7 THE FOUR OPERATIONS OF DECIMALS

1 Addition and Subtraction

David drank 0.7 liter of milk.

John drank 0.2 liter of milk.

(a) How much milk did they drink altogether?

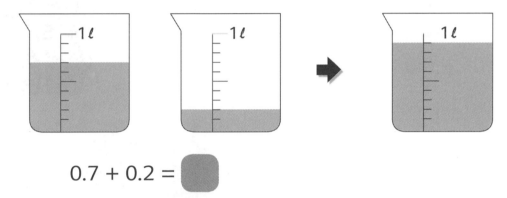

$$0.7 + 0.2 = \boxed{}$$

They drank ⬜ liter of milk altogether.

(b) How much more milk did David drink than John?

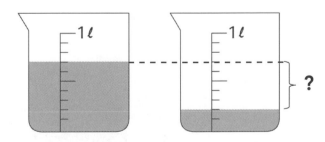

$$0.7 - 0.2 = \boxed{}$$

David drank ⬜ liter more milk than John.

1. (a) Add 0.4 and 0.3.

4 tenths + 3 tenths = 7 tenths

0.4 + 0.3 = ▢

(b) Add 0.04 and 0.03.

4 hundredths +
3 hundredths =
7 hundredths

0.04 + 0.03 = ▢

2. Add 0.7 and 0.6.

$$
\begin{array}{r}
0\,.\,7 \\
+\quad 0\,.\,6 \\
\hline
1\,.\,3
\end{array}
$$

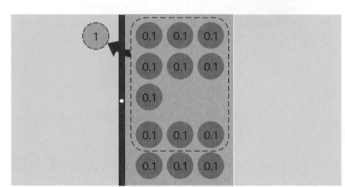

3. Add 0.07 and 0.06.

$$
\begin{array}{r}
0\,.\,0\,7 \\
+\quad 0\,.\,0\,6 \\
\hline
0\,.\,1\,3
\end{array}
$$

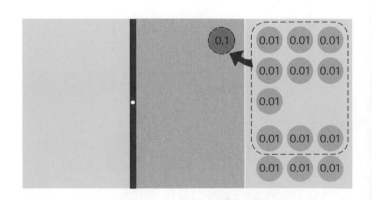

4. Find the value of each of the following.

    (a) 0.6 + 0.2   (b) 0.8 + 0.5   (c) 0.3 + 0.9
    (d) 0.02 + 0.04   (e) 0.07 + 0.03   (f) 0.08 + 0.09

 Exercise 1, page 42

5. Add 6.9 and 0.4.

   6.9 + 0.4 = 6 + 1.3

          = ▢

6.9 + 0.4

6   0.9

0.9 + 0.4 = 1.3

6. Add 3.6 and 1.8.

     3 . 6
 +   1 . 8
   ▢

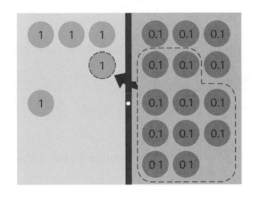

Add the tenths.

$$\begin{array}{r} {}^{1}\,3 . 6 \\ +\ \ 1 . 8 \\ \hline 4 \end{array}$$

Add the ones.

$$\begin{array}{r} {}^{1}\,3 . 6 \\ +\ \ 1 . 8 \\ \hline 5 . 4 \end{array}$$

7. Find the value of each of the following.

    (a) 8 + 0.5   (b) 2.8 + 0.7   (c) 3.4 + 0.6

    (d) 2.6 + 7   (e) 3.7 + 2.3   (f) 4.9 + 1.8

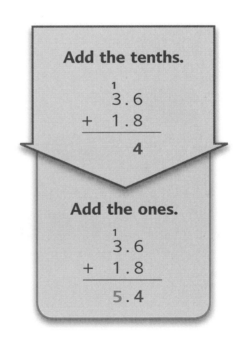 Exercise 2, page 43

8. (a) Add 0.42 and 0.9.

$$0.42 + 0.9 = 0.02 + 1.3$$

$$= \quad \boxed{}$$

$$0.42 + 0.9$$
$$\diagup \quad \diagdown$$
$$0.4 \quad 0.02$$
$$0.4 + 0.9 = 1.3$$

(b) Add 0.42 and 0.09.

$$0.42 + 0.09 = 0.4 + 0.11$$

$$= \quad \boxed{}$$

$$0.42 + 0.09$$
$$\diagup \quad \diagdown$$
$$0.4 \quad 0.02$$
$$0.02 + 0.09 = 0.11$$

9. Add 0.24 and 0.37.

$$
\begin{array}{r}
0.24 \\
+\ \ 0.37 \\
\hline
\end{array}
$$
$$\boxed{}$$

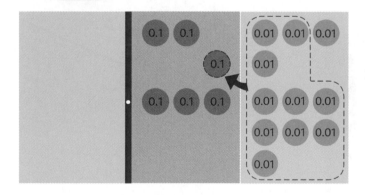

Add the hundredths.

$$
\begin{array}{r}
\overset{1}{0}.24 \\
+\ \ 0.37 \\
\hline
1
\end{array}
$$

Add the tenths.

$$
\begin{array}{r}
\overset{1}{0}.24 \\
+\ \ 0.37 \\
\hline
0.61
\end{array}
$$

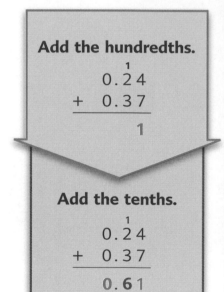

10. Find the value of each of the following.

(a) 0.63 + 2   (b) 0.56 + 0.4   (c) 0.84 + 0.3
(d) 6 + 0.02   (e) 0.37 + 0.03   (f) 0.97 + 0.06
(g) 4 + 0.28   (h) 0.65 + 0.53   (i) 0.86 + 0.49
(j) 1.49 + 6   (k) 2.46 + 0.6   (l) 3.94 + 0.06

11. Add 2.63 and 3.84.

$$
\begin{array}{r}
2.63 \\
+\ \ 3.84 \\
\hline
\end{array}
$$

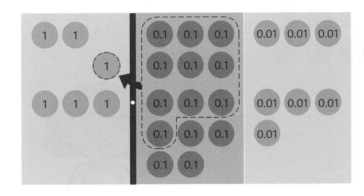

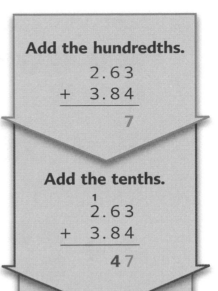

Add the hundredths.

$$
\begin{array}{r}
2.63 \\
+\ \ 3.84 \\
\hline
7
\end{array}
$$

Add the tenths.

$$
\begin{array}{r}
{\scriptstyle 1} \\
2.63 \\
+\ \ 3.84 \\
\hline
47
\end{array}
$$

Add the ones.

$$
\begin{array}{r}
{\scriptstyle 1} \\
2.63 \\
+\ \ 3.84 \\
\hline
6.47
\end{array}
$$

Exercise 3, pages 44-45

12. Estimate the value of 34.26 + 10.82.

34 + 11 = 45

13. For each of the following, estimate the value. Then add.

Are the answers reasonable?

(a) 25.48 and 7.64

$$
\begin{array}{r}
25.48 \\
+\ \ 7.64 \\
\hline
\end{array}
$$

(b) 4.8 and 2.37

$$
\begin{array}{r}
4.80 \\
+\ \ 2.37 \\
\hline
\end{array}
$$

14. For each of the following, estimate the value. Then add.

(a) 2.96 + 6.8   (b) 3.64 + 2.7   (c) 3.2 + 3.98
(d) 3.54 + 2.38   (e) 6.57 + 2.86   (f) 8.92 + 4.16

Exercise 4, page 46

15. (a) Subtract 0.2 from 0.8.

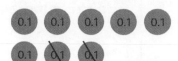

8 tenths — 2 tenths = 6 tenths

0.8 − 0.2 = ⬜

(b) Subtract 0.2 from 1.

1 one = 10 tenths
10 tenths − 2 tenths
= 8 tenths

1 − 0.2 = ⬜

(c) Subtract 0.2 from 3.

3 − 0.2 = ⬜

16. Subtract 0.8 from 4.2.

$$\begin{array}{r} \overset{3}{\cancel{4}}.\overset{12}{\cancel{2}} \\ -\ \ 0.8 \\ \hline 3.4 \end{array}$$

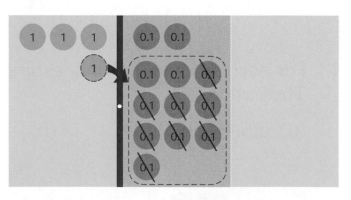

17. Find the value of each of the following.

(a) 0.5 − 0.3   (b) 0.7 − 0.5   (c) 0.9 − 0.2
(d) 1 − 0.4   (e) 2 − 0.7   (f) 4 − 0.9
(g) 1.4 − 0.8   (h) 4.7 − 0.6   (i) 5.3 − 0.9
(j) 0.58 − 0.3   (k) 4.05 − 0.5   (l) 5.12 − 0.4

40

Exercise 5, page 47

18. (a) Subtract 0.06 from 0.08.

8 hundredths
− 6 hundredths
= 2 hundredths

0.08 − 0.06 = ▢

(b) Subtract 0.06 from 0.1.

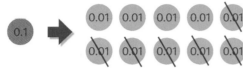

0.1 − 0.06 = ▢

(c) Subtract 0.06 from 1.

1 tenth = 10 hundredths

1 − 0.06 = ▢

19. Subtract 0.23 from 1.

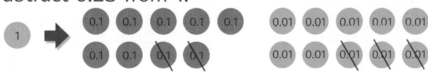

1 one = 9 tenths
10 hundredths

1 − 0.23 = ▢

20. Find the value of each of the following.

(a) 0.09 − 0.02   (b) 0.49 − 0.02   (c) 3.49 − 0.02
(d) 0.1 − 0.04   (e) 0.3 − 0.04   (f) 2.3 − 0.04
(g) 1 − 0.07   (h) 2 − 0.07   (i) 4 − 0.09
(j) 1 − 0.45   (k) 3 − 0.45   (l) 4 − 0.86

21. Subtract 0.08 from 4.2.

$$\begin{array}{r} \overset{1\ \ \ \ 10}{4.2\cancel{0}} \\ -\ \ 0.08 \\ \hline 4.12 \end{array}$$

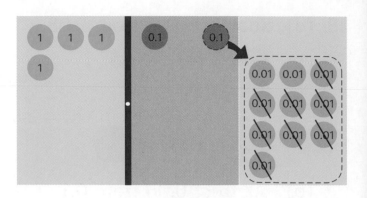

22. Find the value of each of the following.

(a) 3.29 − 0.06   (b) 3.54 − 0.07   (c) 4.25 − 0.09
(d) 4.8 − 0.06   (e) 6.2 − 0.07   (f) 6.5 − 0.09

Exercise 6, pages 48-49

23. Subtract 2.7 from 6.

$$\begin{array}{r} \overset{5\ \ \ \ 10}{\cancel{6}.\cancel{0}} \\ -\ \ 2.7 \\ \hline \end{array}$$

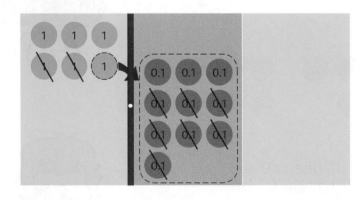

Subtract the tenths.

$$\begin{array}{r} \overset{5\ \ \ \ 10}{\cancel{6}.\cancel{0}} \\ -\ \ 2.7 \\ \hline 3 \end{array}$$

Subtract the ones.

$$\begin{array}{r} \overset{5\ \ \ \ 10}{\cancel{6}.\cancel{0}} \\ -\ \ 2.7 \\ \hline 3.3 \end{array}$$

24. Find the value of each of the following.

(a) 4.9 − 1.3   (b) 5.2 − 1.7   (c) 5.5 − 2.8
(d) 4.1 − 1.6   (e) 5 − 2.4   (f) 8 − 3.2

Exercise 7, page 50

25. Subtract 2.53 from 4.27.

$$\begin{array}{r} 4.27 \\ -\ 2.53 \\ \hline \end{array}$$

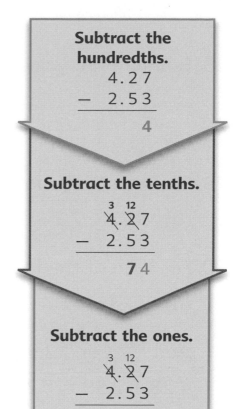

Subtract the hundredths.

$$\begin{array}{r} 4.27 \\ -\ 2.53 \\ \hline 4 \end{array}$$

Subtract the tenths.

$$\begin{array}{r} {}^{3}\ {}^{12} \\ \cancel{4}.\cancel{2}7 \\ -\ 2.53 \\ \hline 74 \end{array}$$

Subtract the ones.

$$\begin{array}{r} {}^{3}\ {}^{12} \\ \cancel{4}.\cancel{2}7 \\ -\ 2.53 \\ \hline 1.74 \end{array}$$

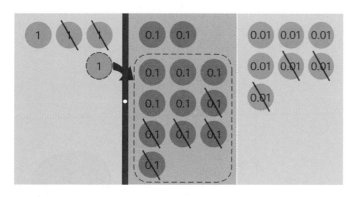

26. Subtract.

(a) $7.24 - 3.5 =$ ☐

$$\begin{array}{r} 7.24 \\ -\ 3.50 \\ \hline \end{array}$$

(b) $0.8 - 0.49 =$ ☐

$$\begin{array}{r} 0.80 \\ -\ 0.49 \\ \hline \end{array}$$

(c) $5 - 1.27 =$ ☐

$$\begin{array}{r} 5.00 \\ -\ 1.27 \\ \hline \end{array}$$

(d) $6.2 - 3.54 =$ ☐

$$\begin{array}{r} 6.20 \\ -\ 3.54 \\ \hline \end{array}$$

27. Find the value of each of the following.

(a) $0.85 - 0.43$ (b) $0.64 - 0.39$ (c) $1.54 - 0.66$
(d) $4.72 - 1.32$ (e) $5.87 - 2.38$ (f) $6.05 - 2.5$
(g) $0.6 - 0.16$ (h) $2.9 - 0.75$ (i) $2.1 - 0.48$
(j) $3.4 - 1.85$ (k) $6 - 2.56$ (l) $4.5 - 3.55$

Exercise 8, pages 51-52

28. Estimate the value of 27.82 − 8.3. $28 − 8 = 20$

29. For each of the following, estimate the value. Then add.

   (a) 8.67 + 7.2　　(b) 42.36 + 7.65　　(c) 20.81 + 18.76

30. For each of the following, estimate the value. Then subtract.

   (a) 7.23 − 4.6　　(b) 30.45 − 8.56　　(c) 52.36 − 24.82

31. Add 4.28 and 2.99.

   4.28 + 2.99 = 7.28 − 0.01

 = 　　　　$4.28 + 3 = 7.28$

32. Add 8.99 and 0.99.

   8.99 + 0.99 = 10 − 0.02

   = 　　　　$9 + 1 = 10$

33. Subtract 1.99 from 5.62.

   5.62 − 1.99 = 3.62 + 0.01

   = 　　　　$5.62 − 2 = 3.62$

34. Find the value of each of the following.

   (a) 3.87 + 1.99　　(b) 2.99 + 7.81　　(c) 3.99 + 5.99
   (d) 4.52 − 0.99　　(e) 5.03 − 2.99　　(f) 8.1 − 3.99

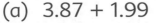

44

Exercise 9, page 53

35. At a store, Mrs. Lee paid $1.75 for a pen, $3.99 for a pair of slippers and $5.40 for a book. How much did she spend altogether?

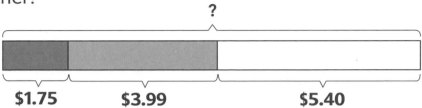

$$\$1.75 + \$3.99 + \$5.40 = \$\boxed{}$$

She spent $\boxed{}$ altogether.

36. Emily has a white ribbon and a blue ribbon. The white ribbon is 1.85 m long. The blue ribbon is 1.4 m longer than the white ribbon. Find the total length of the two ribbons.

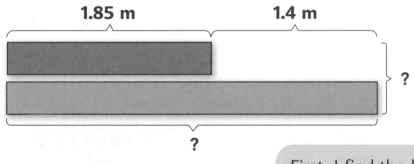

First, I find the length of the blue ribbon.

$$1.85 + 1.4 = 3.25$$

The length of the blue ribbon is 3.25 m.

$$1.85 + 3.25 = \boxed{}$$

The total length is $\boxed{}$ m.

37. Samantha bought a fish for $5.25. She also bought some flowers for $11.80. She paid with a $50 bill. How much change did she receive?

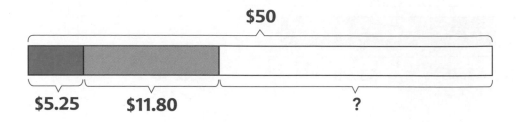

$50

$5.25 $11.80   ?

Method 1:

I subtract $5.25 and $11.80 from $50.

$50 − $5.25 − $11.80 = $⬚

She received $⬚ change.

Method 2:

First, I find the total amount of money Samantha spent.

$5.25 + $11.80 = $17.05

She spent $17.05 altogether.

$50 − $17.05 = $⬚

She received $⬚ change.

Exercise 10, pages 54-56

PRACTICE A

Find the value of each of the following.

	(a)	(b)	(c)
1.	0.5 + 0.4	0.8 + 0.9	3.2 + 0.9
2.	0.02 + 0.08	0.07 + 0.04	0.76 + 0.5
3.	0.9 − 0.8	2 − 0.4	3.2 − 0.6
4.	0.06 − 0.03	1 − 0.07	4 − 0.65
5.	4.7 + 3.6	0.58 + 0.24	0.82 + 1.2
6.	6.8 − 4.3	0.92 − 0.08	1.46 − 0.59

7. Round the numbers to the nearest whole number and then find the value of each of the following.

(a) 2.56 + 6.29   (b) 1.08 + 6.5   (c) 16.39 + 3.65
(d) 3.56 − 0.76   (e) 9.31 − 4.8   (f) 5.62 − 1.98

8. Tracy is 1.32 m tall. She is 0.07 m taller than Brianne. How tall is Brianne?

9. Samantha spent $5.75 on vegetables. She spent $7.50 more on meat than on vegetables. How much did she spend on meat?

10. After spending $3.60, Pablo had $16.80 left. How much money did he have at first?

11. Nathan's weight was 42.5 kg three years ago. Now he weighs 38.6 kg. How much weight did he lose?

12. Fred's time in a race was 14.5 seconds. Jordan's time was 15.3 seconds. Who ran faster and how much faster?

PRACTICE B

Find the value of each of the following.

	(a)	(b)	(c)
1.	40.23 + 8.45	18.06 + 1.37	26.29 + 13.73
2.	24.9 + 3.7	10.99 + 6.32	12.99 + 6.99
3.	13.58 − 0.25	24.5 − 2.27	17.02 − 12.13
4.	39.45 − 2.8	16.04 − 4.99	25.6 − 14.99

5. A pineapple weighs 1.69 lb. A watermelon is 2.51 lb heavier than the pineapple. What is the total weight of the two fruits?

6. Kate bought 3 liters of milk. She drank 0.5 liter and gave 0.25 liter to her cat. How many liters of milk did she have left?

7. Mitchell jogged 5.85 km on Saturday. He jogged 1.7 km less on Sunday than on Saturday. What was the total distance he jogged on the two days?

8. After using 24.8 cm of ribbon to tie a present and 12.6 cm to make a bow, Annie had 18.4 cm of ribbon left. How many centimeters of ribbon did she have at first?

9. Morgan, Annie and Lucy went shopping and spent a total of $15. Morgan spent $4.15 and Annie spent $6.80. How much did Lucy spend?

10. Mrs. Bates bought a bottle of apple juice for $4.90 and 1 kg of grapes for $7.50. She gave the cashier $15. How much change did she receive?

❷ Multiplication

Jean drinks 0.4 liter of milk a day.

How many liters of milk does she drink in 3 days?

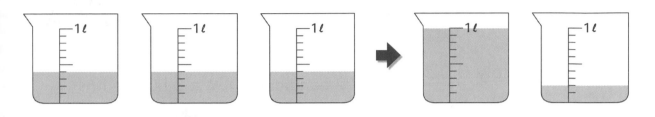

$0.4 \times 3 = $ ⬜

She drinks ⬜ liters of milk in 3 days.

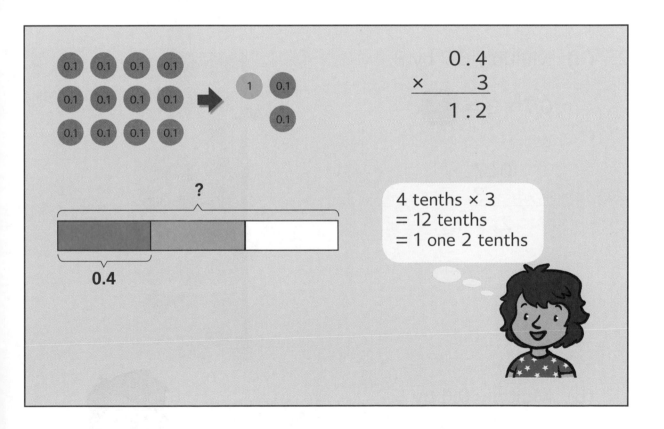

$$\begin{array}{r} 0.4 \\ \times\quad 3 \\ \hline 1.2 \end{array}$$

4 tenths × 3
= 12 tenths
= 1 one 2 tenths

0.4

1. (a) Multiply 0.2 by 4.

$0.2 \times 4 =$

2 tenths × 4 = 8 tenths

(b) Multiply 0.02 by 4.

2 hundredths × 4 = 8 hundredths

0.01 0.01 0.01 0.01
0.01 0.01 0.01 0.01

$0.02 \times 4 =$

2. (a) Multiply 0.7 by 3.

$0.7 \times 3 =$

$$\begin{array}{r} 0.7 \\ \times \quad 3 \\ \hline 2.1 \end{array}$$

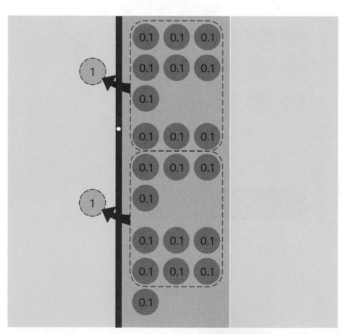

(b) Multiply 0.6 by 5.

$0.6 \times 5 =$

6 tenths × 5
= 30 tenths
= 3 ones

3. (a) Multiply 0.07 by 3.

$0.07 \times 3 =$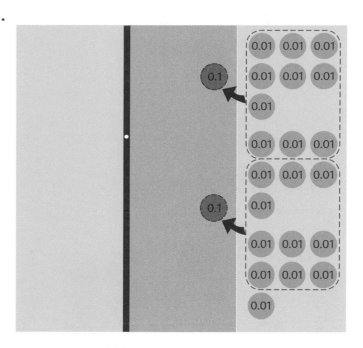

(b) Multiply 0.06 by 5.

$0.06 \times 5 =$

6 hundredths × 5
= 30 hundredths
= 3 tenths

4. Find the product of each of the following.

(a) 3×2 (b) 0.3×2 (c) 0.03×2
(d) 4×7 (e) 0.4×7 (f) 0.04×7
(g) 5×8 (h) 0.5×8 (i) 0.05×8

5. Multiply $0.80 by 4.

$0.80 \times 4 = \$$

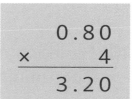

```
    0.80
×      4
    3.20
```

6. Find the value of each of the following.

(a) 0.20×4 (b) 0.60×7 (c) 0.90×8

Exercise 11, pages 57-58

7. Multiply 4.3 by 3.

$4.3 \times 3 =$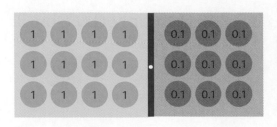

8. Multiply 20.7 by 6.

$20.7 \times 6 =$

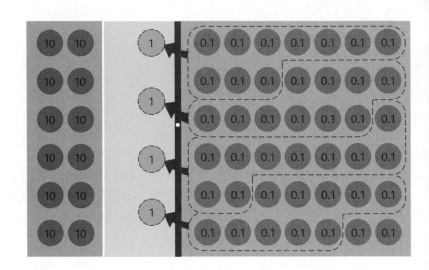

$$\begin{array}{r} 2\,0\,.\,7 \\ \times \qquad 6 \\ \hline \end{array}$$

9. Estimate the value of 21.2 × 6.

$20 \times 6 = 120$

10. For each of the following, estimate the product.
Then multiply.

(a) 5.9 × 2   (b) 3.9 × 5   (c) 8 × 32.6
(d) 18.5 × 2   (e) 3 × 26.8   (f) 130.2 × 4

Exercise 12, page 59

11. Multiply 0.25 by 3.

$$
\begin{array}{r}
0.25 \\
\times \quad 3 \\
\hline
\end{array}
$$

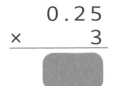

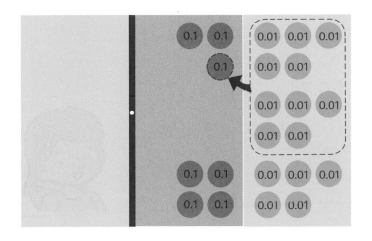

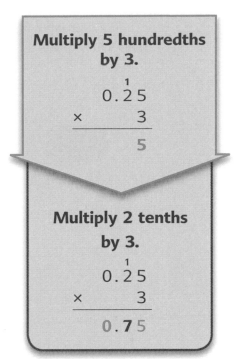

Multiply 5 hundredths by 3.

$$
\begin{array}{r}
\overset{1}{0.2}5 \\
\times \quad 3 \\
\hline
5
\end{array}
$$

Multiply 2 tenths by 3.

$$
\begin{array}{r}
\overset{1}{0.2}5 \\
\times \quad 3 \\
\hline
0.75
\end{array}
$$

12. Multiply 4.53 by 2.

$$
\begin{array}{r}
4.53 \\
\times \quad 2 \\
\hline
\end{array}
$$

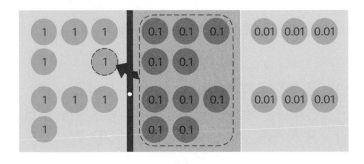

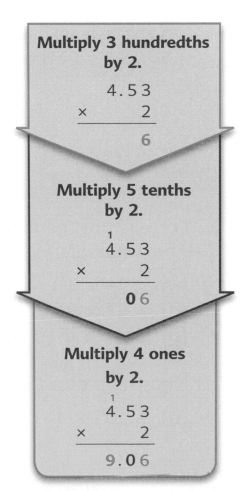

Multiply 3 hundredths by 2.

$$
\begin{array}{r}
4.53 \\
\times \quad 2 \\
\hline
6
\end{array}
$$

Multiply 5 tenths by 2.

$$
\begin{array}{r}
\overset{1}{4.5}3 \\
\times \quad 2 \\
\hline
06
\end{array}
$$

Multiply 4 ones by 2.

$$
\begin{array}{r}
\overset{1}{4.5}3 \\
\times \quad 2 \\
\hline
9.06
\end{array}
$$

13. Multiply.

    (a) $46.01 \times 9 =$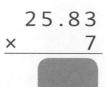

$$
\begin{array}{r}
4\,6\,.\,0\,1 \\
\times \qquad 9 \\
\hline
\end{array}
$$

    (b) $7 \times 25.83 =$

$$
\begin{array}{r}
2\,5\,.\,8\,3 \\
\times \qquad 7 \\
\hline
\end{array}
$$

14. Estimate the product of 6.84×9.

$7 \times 9 = 63$

15. Estimate the product of 0.42×8.

0.42 is less than one half.
So 0.42×8 will be less than half of 8.

$0.4 \times 8 = 3.2$

16. For each of the following, estimate the product.
Then multiply.

    (a) 0.26×4 (b) 3.12×4 (c) 0.45×4
    (d) 4.52×8 (e) 34.02×3 (f) 48.26×6
    (g) 5×36.15 (h) 8×55.25 (i) 29.73×7

17. Find the product of each of the following.

    (a) $\$2.05 \times 4$ (b) $\$19.50 \times 6$ (c) $\$32.45 \times 9$

Exercise 13, pages 60-61

18. Jared sold 6 books at $3.95 each. How much money did he collect altogether?

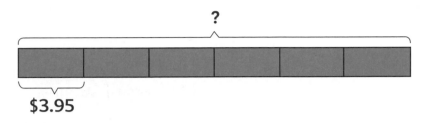

$3.95 × 6 = $ ◯

He collected $ ◯ altogether.

19. Rachel saved $20.05. Susan saved 4 times as much as Rachel. How much did Susan save?

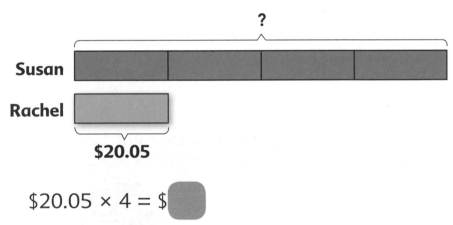

$20.05 × 4 = $ ◯

Susan saved $ ◯.

20. Sam had $30. He bought 4 sets of stamps from a post office. Each set of stamps cost $2.95. How much money did he have left?

First, I find the total cost of 4 sets of stamps.

$2.95 × 4 = $11.80

4 sets of stamps cost $11.80.

$30 − $11.80 = $ ⬚

He had $ ⬚ left.

21. Sophie bought some material to make 6 curtains. She used 3.15 m for each curtain. She had 2.5 m of material left after making the curtains. How many meters of material did she buy?

First, I find the total length of material used.

3.15 × 6 = 18.9

She used 18.9 m of material.

18.9 + 2.5 = ⬚

She bought ⬚ m of material.

Exercise 14, pages 62-64

PRACTICE C

Find the value of each of the following.

	(a)	(b)	(c)
1.	2.5 + 6.1	4.2 + 6.8	1.38 + 0.9
2.	2.7 + 3.53	2.45 + 2.07	3.18 + 0.96
3.	7.8 − 2.5	8.2 − 4.7	4.6 − 2.75
4.	5 − 3.48	9.05 − 5.88	7.21 − 4.36
5.	0.4 × 9	7 × 0.8	0.31 × 6
6.	3 × 0.45	1.5 × 4	3.86 × 5

7. Estimate and then multiply.

   (a) 3.2 × 6   (b) 2.48 × 3   (c) 4.09 × 5

8. In a high jump event, Cameron cleared 1.5 m and Jordan cleared 1.39 m. Find the difference between the two results.

9. A worker mixed 13.45 lb of cement with sand. The weight of sand used was 3 times the weight of the cement. How many pounds of sand did he use?

10. Mrs. Lee bought 4 packets of spices and a can of cocoa. Each packet of spices costs $0.85 and the can of cocoa costs $3.75. How much did she spend altogether?

11. A painter mixed 1.46 liters of black paint with 0.8 liter of white paint to get gray paint. Then he used 0.96 liter of the gray paint. How much gray paint did he have left?

12. Mrs. Bates bought 5 pots of plant. Each pot of plant cost $2.35. She gave the cashier $20. How much change did she receive?

③ Division

Barry poured 0.9 liter of water equally into 3 beakers.
How much water was there in each beaker?

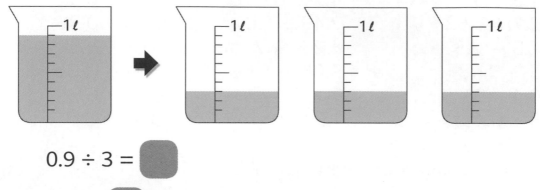

$0.9 \div 3 =$ ⬜

There was ⬜ liter of water in each beaker.

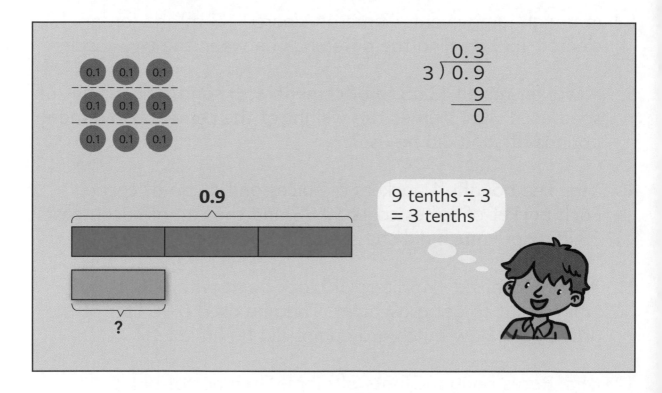

9 tenths ÷ 3
= 3 tenths

1. (a) Divide 0.6 by 2.

6 tenths ÷ 2
= 3 tenths

0.6 ÷ 2 = ▢

(b) Divide 0.06 by 2.

6 hundredths ÷ 2
= 3 hundredths

0.06 ÷ 2 = ▢

2. (a) Divide 1.8 by 3.

1.8 ÷ 3 = ▢

18 tenths ÷ 3
= 6 tenths

$$\begin{array}{r} 0.6 \\ 3\overline{)1.8} \\ 1.8 \\ \hline 0 \end{array}$$

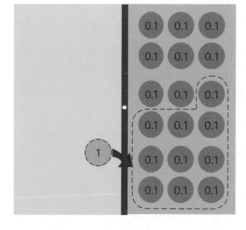

(b) Divide 2 by 4.

2 ÷ 4 = ▢

20 tenths ÷ 4
= 5 tenths

3. (a) Divide 0.18 by 3.

18 hundredths ÷ 3
= 6 hundredths

0.18 ÷ 3 =

$$
\begin{array}{r}
0.06 \\
3\overline{)0.18} \\
\underline{18} \\
0
\end{array}
$$

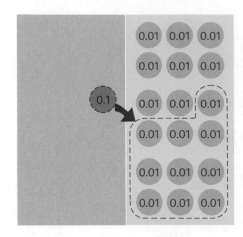

(b) Divide 0.2 by 4.

20 hundredths ÷ 4
= 5 hundredths

0.2 ÷ 4 =

4. Find the value of each of the following.

(a) 8 ÷ 4   (b) 0.8 ÷ 4   (c) 0.08 ÷ 4
(d) 35 ÷ 7   (e) 3.5 ÷ 7   (f) 0.35 ÷ 7
(g) 30 ÷ 5   (h) 3 ÷ 5   (i) 0.3 ÷ 5

5. Divide $4.20 by 6.

$4.20 ÷ 6 = $

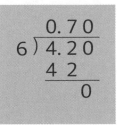

$$
\begin{array}{r}
0.70 \\
6\overline{)4.20} \\
\underline{4\,2} \\
0
\end{array}
$$

6. Find the value of each of the following.

(a) $0.90 ÷ 3   (b) $2.40 ÷ 8   (c) $5.40 ÷ 9

Exercise 15, pages 65-66

7. Divide 0.74 by 2.

2$\overline{)0.74}$

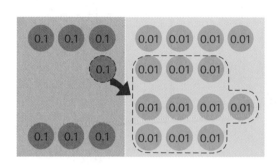

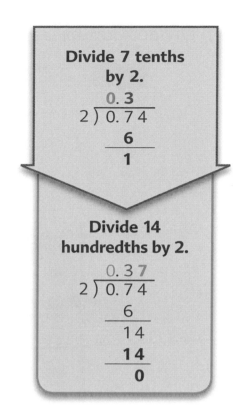

Divide 7 tenths by 2.

$$\begin{array}{r} 0.3 \\ 2\overline{)0.74} \\ 6 \\ \hline 1 \end{array}$$

Divide 14 hundredths by 2.

$$\begin{array}{r} 0.37 \\ 2\overline{)0.74} \\ 6 \\ \hline 14 \\ 14 \\ \hline 0 \end{array}$$

8. Find the value of each of the following.

   (a) 0.39 ÷ 3   (b) 0.84 ÷ 4   (c) 0.77 ÷ 7
   (d) 0.68 ÷ 4   (e) 0.75 ÷ 5   (f) 0.96 ÷ 6

9. Divide $0.60 by 4.

   $0.60 ÷ 4 = $

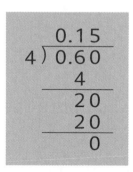

$$\begin{array}{r} 0.15 \\ 4\overline{)0.60} \\ 4 \\ \hline 20 \\ 20 \\ \hline 0 \end{array}$$

10. Find the value of each of the following.

   (a) $0.30 ÷ 2   (b) $0.45 ÷ 3   (c) $0.95 ÷ 5

Exercise 16, page 67

11. Divide 4.35 by 3.

$$3 \overline{)4.35}$$

Divide 4 ones by 3.

$$\begin{array}{r} 1 \\ 3\overline{)4.35} \\ \underline{3} \\ 1 \end{array}$$

Divide 13 tenths by 3.

$$\begin{array}{r} 1.4 \\ 3\overline{)4.35} \\ \underline{3} \\ 13 \\ \underline{12} \\ 1 \end{array}$$

Divide 15 hundredths by 3.

$$\begin{array}{r} 1.45 \\ 3\overline{)4.35} \\ \underline{3} \\ 13 \\ \underline{12} \\ 15 \\ \underline{15} \\ 0 \end{array}$$

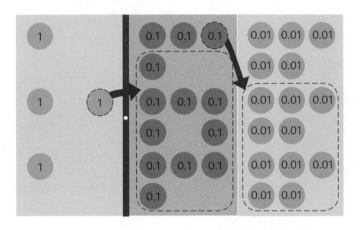

12. Estimate the value of 31.2 ÷ 8.

32 ÷ 8 = 4

13. Estimate the value of 5.28 ÷ 6.

5.4 ÷ 6 = 0.9

14. For each of the following, estimate the value. Then divide.

(a) 0.81 ÷ 3 (b) 7.12 ÷ 8 (c) 46.35 ÷ 9
(d) 3.96 ÷ 3 (e) 4.12 ÷ 4 (f) 14.58 ÷ 6

15. Divide $18.40 by 8.

$$\$18.40 \div 8 = \$\boxed{}$$

```
      2 . 3 0
8 ) 1 8 . 4 0
    1 6
      2 4
      2 4
        0
```

16. Find the value of each of the following.

(a) $4.65 ÷ 3   (b) $16.50 ÷ 6   (c) $31.05 ÷ 9
(d) $3.55 ÷ 5   (e) $4.32 ÷ 6   (f) $5.04 ÷ 9

Exercise 17, pages 68-70

17. Divide.

(a) $5 \div 4 = \boxed{}$

Divide 5 ones by 4.

```
    1
4 ) 5
    4
    1
```

Divide 10 tenths by 4.

```
    1 . 2
4 ) 5 . 0
    4
    1 0
      8
      2
```

Divide 20 hundredths by 4.

```
    1 . 2 5
4 ) 5 . 0 0
    4
    1 0
      8
      2 0
      2 0
        0
```

(b) $8.1 \div 6 = \boxed{}$

Divide 8 ones by 6.

```
    1
6 ) 8 . 1
    6
    2
```

Divide 21 tenths by 6.

```
    1 . 3
6 ) 8 . 1
    6
    2 1
    1 8
      3
```

Divide 30 hundredths by 6.

```
    1 . 3 5
6 ) 8 . 1 0
    6
    2 1
    1 8
      3 0
      3 0
        0
```

18. Divide.

(a) 30.4 ÷ 5 =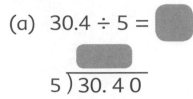

$$5\overline{)30.40}$$

(b) 12 ÷ 8 = ▢

$$8\overline{)12.0}$$

19. Find the value of each of the following.

(a) 8 ÷ 5   (b) 15 ÷ 6   (c) 22 ÷ 8
(d) 0.9 ÷ 2   (e) 1.7 ÷ 5   (f) 25.5 ÷ 6

Exercise 18, pages 71-72

20. Find the value of 7 ÷ 3 correct to 1 decimal place.

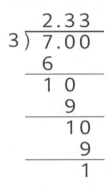

$$
\begin{array}{r}
2.33 \\
3\overline{)7.00} \\
6 \\
\hline
1\ 0 \\
9 \\
\hline
1\,0 \\
9 \\
\hline
1
\end{array}
$$

Divide to 2 decimal places. Then round the answer to 1 decimal place.

2.33 is ▢ when rounded to 1 decimal place.

7 ÷ 3 = ▢ (1 decimal place)

21. Find the value of 78.5 ÷ 4 correct to 1 decimal place.

78.5 ÷ 4 = ▢ (1 decimal place)

22. Find the value of each of the following correct to
1 decimal place.

(a) 1 ÷ 6   (b) 4 ÷ 7   (c) 5 ÷ 9
(d) 0.9 ÷ 4   (e) 2.5 ÷ 6   (f) 43.5 ÷ 8

Exercise 19, page 73

23. Ellie bought 5 packets of dates for $8.
How much did two packets cost?

$8

?

$8 ÷ 5 = $1.60

First, I find the
cost of each packet.

Each packet cost $1.60.
Two packets cost $1.60 × 2 = $ ⬜

24. Taylor has $5.40.
He has 3 times as much money as Bonita.
How much more money does Taylor have than Bonita?

$5.40

Taylor

Bonita

?   ?

$5.40 ÷ 3 = $1.80

First, I find the amount
of money Bonita has.

Bonita has $1.80.

$5.40 − $1.80 = $ ⬜

Taylor has $ ⬜ more than Bonita.

25. Steve bought 5 gal of orange juice. After filling up 5 bottles of the same size with the orange juice, he had 0.25 gal of orange juice left. Find the amount of orange juice in each bottle.

First, I find the total amount of orange juice in 5 bottles.

$5 - 0.25 = 4.75$

The total amount of orange juice in 5 bottles was 4.75 gal.

$4.75 \div 5 =$

The amount of orange juice in each bottle was ☐ gal.

26. Mrs. Kim used 4 bags of flour to make 5 cakes of the same size. Each bag of flour weighed 1.35 kg. How much flour did she use for each cake?

$1.35 \times 4 = 5.4$

4 bags of flour weighed 5.4 kg.

$5.4 \div 5 =$

She used ☐ kg of flour for each cake.

Exercise 20, pages 74-76

PRACTICE D

Find the value of each of the following.

	(a)	(b)	(c)
1.	4 × 8.2	5.29 × 3	8 × 3.29
2.	$0.15 × 6	$4.05 × 4	$3.40 × 9
3.	25.6 ÷ 8	2.94 ÷ 7	6.8 ÷ 5
4.	$0.90 ÷ 6	$4.20 ÷ 7	$6.80 ÷ 8

5. For each of the following, estimate the product. Then multiply.

   (a) 9 × 4.36   (b) 6 × 5.25   (c) 1.94 × 7

6. For each of the following, estimate the value. Then divide.

   (a) 5.9 ÷ 2   (b) 23.94 ÷ 6   (c) 35.04 ÷ 4

7. Mrs. King poured 6 qt of syrup equally into 4 bottles. How much syrup was there in each bottle?

8. 1 liter of gas weighs 1.25 kg. What is the weight of 6 liters of gas?

9. A ribbon 6.75 yd long is cut into 5 equal pieces. How long is each piece?

10. Dan spent $3 on string and $1.40 on beads to make one pot hanger. How much will it cost him to make 4 pot hangers?

11. When a box contains 6 bars of chocolate, it weighs 2.34 kg. The box, when empty, weighs 0.06 kg. Find the weight of one bar of chocolate.

12. Maria paid $8.25 for a book and a comic. The book cost twice as much as the comic. Find the cost of the book.

1. Steve used 8 cans of paint to paint his home. Each can contained 5.5 liters of paint. How much paint did he use altogether?

2. Mrs. Wells weighs 47.6 kg. She is 4 times as heavy as her daughter. What is her daughter's weight?

3. A doll costs $4.95. A toy robot costs 3 times as much as the doll. Find the cost of the toy robot.

4. 3 girls shared the cost of a birthday present equally. The birthday present cost $17.40. How much did each girl pay?

5. Mr. Friedman bought 5 storybooks at $2.80 each. He gave the cashier $20. How much change did he receive?

6. Marvin bought 5 m of cloth at a sale. He gave the cashier $50 and received $15.25 change. Find the cost of 1 m of cloth.

7. Mary saved $25 in 5 days. She saved $4.60 a day in the first 4 days. How much did she save on the fifth day?

8. 3 cups of tea and a glass of orange juice cost $4.40. Each cup of tea costs $0.65. Find the cost of the glass of orange juice.

PRACTICE F

1. Eric and his friends had 3 plates of pasta for lunch. Each plate of pasta cost $2.50. How much did they pay altogether?

2. Mrs. Moss used 6.6 m of lace for 4 pillow cases. If she used an equal length of lace for each pillow case, how much lace did she use for each pillow case?

3. Damon mailed 4 packages. One of them weighed 1.8 kg. The other 3 packages weighed 2.05 kg each. Find the total weight of the 4 packages.

4. Tracy bought a teapot and 6 cups. The teapot cost $5.65. Each cup cost $1.45. How much did she spend altogether?

5. Natalie and Alice shared the cost of their lunch equally. The lunch cost $6.70. How much money did Alice have left if she had $15.35 at first?

6. Janet bought 3 pencils and a pen for $2.20. If the pen cost $0.85, how much did each pencil cost?

7. Mrs. Dunn sewed curtains for her living room and 3 bedrooms. She used 3.46 m of material for each bedroom and 4.25 m of material for the living room. How much material did she use altogether?

8. The usual price of an apple is $0.60. At a sale, a bag of 4 apples is sold for $2.20. How much cheaper is an apple at the sale?

REVIEW 7

1. (a) What number is 0.1 more than 124.56?
   (b) What number is 0.01 more than 124.56?
   (c) What number is 0.1 less than 124.56?
   (d) What number is 0.01 less than 124.56?

2. Replace each ● with >, < or =.

   (a) $4\frac{3}{5}$ ● 4.35

   (b) $2\frac{2}{50}$ ● 2.2

   (c) 14.09 ● $14\frac{1}{10}$

   (d) $7\frac{3}{20}$ ● 7.15

3. Write the missing number in each ■.

   (a) $4.12 = 4 + \frac{1}{10} + \frac{2}{■}$

   (b) $1.08 = \frac{■}{100}$

   (c) $5.7 = 5 + \frac{7}{■}$

   (d) $39.16 = 39 + \frac{■}{10} + \frac{6}{100}$

4. Find the value of each of the following.

   (a) $\frac{1}{4}$ of $140

   (b) $\frac{1}{3}$ of 27 kg

   (c) $\frac{1}{5}$ of 50 m

5. For each of the following, estimate the product. Then multiply.

   (a) 8.9 × 7

   (b) 3.99 × 5

   (c) 10.99 × 3

6. What is the value of the digit **8** in each of the following?

   (a) **38**,157   (b) 45**8**3   (c) 12,43**8**   (d) **8**9,015

7. Arrange the following numbers in order from the smallest.

   2,   −6,   20,   −30

8. Which one of the following has 6 as a factor?

   61,   36,   56,   76

9. The diameter of a circle is twice as long as its .

A diameter passes through the of a circle.

The length of a radius is ▢ cm when the diameter is 20 cm.

10. What is the value of n in each of the following?

(a) $35 - 15 \div 5 = n - 3$ (b) $123 \div 2 = 61 + n$

(c) $50 = (2 \times n) \times 2$ (d) $n \times 100 = 23{,}800$

(e) $36 \times 25 = n \times 4 \times 25$ (f) $\frac{5}{8} + \frac{n}{16} = 1$

(g) $3\frac{1}{8} = 2 + n$

11. The product of two numbers is 456.
    If one of the numbers is 8, what is the other number?

12. Find the sum of each of the following.

(a) $\frac{1}{3}$ and $\frac{9}{12}$ (b) $\frac{1}{3}$ and $\frac{5}{9}$

(c) $\frac{5}{6}$ and $\frac{1}{2}$ (d) $\frac{4}{5}$ and $\frac{7}{10}$

13. Find the difference between each of the following.

(a) $\frac{11}{12}$ and $\frac{1}{4}$ (b) 3 and $\frac{3}{7}$

(c) $\frac{1}{2}$ and $\frac{1}{8}$ (d) 6 and $\frac{1}{6}$

14. Arrange each of the following numbers in increasing order.

(a) $\frac{1}{3}, \frac{5}{6}, \frac{1}{12}$ (b) $1\frac{3}{4}, \frac{9}{4}, 1\frac{1}{4}$

(c) $1\frac{3}{5}, \frac{9}{2}, 3$ (d) $2\frac{1}{5}, \frac{9}{4}, \frac{20}{6}$

15. What type of quadrilateral is formed by the overlap when a triangular-shaped sheet of paper is put on top of a rectangular-shaped sheet of paper as shown?

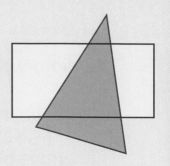

16. The figure below shows a solid.

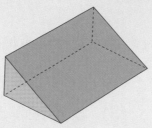

Which one of the following given below is a net of the solid?

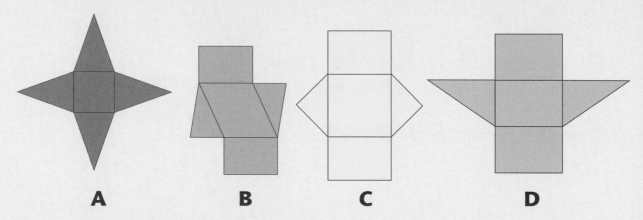

A   B   C   D

17. Mr. Reed sold his car for $35,950. Round this amount of money to the nearest $100.

18. David bought a vacuum cleaner for $76.90. Round this amount of money to the nearest dollar.

19. Divide. Give each answer as a decimal correct to 1 decimal place.

(a) 20 ÷ 3   (b) 100 ÷ 7   (c) 39 ÷ 8

20. The area of a rectangle is 50 cm². If the length of the rectangle is 10 cm, find its width.

21. The perimeter of a square is 36 in. Find the length of one side of the square.

22. A ribbon 34 yards long is cut into 8 equal pieces. How many yards is each piece?

23. A cup of coffee cost $0.65. David ordered 6 cups of coffee. How much did he pay?

24. A ribbon 4.8 m long is cut into 8 equal pieces. What is the length of each piece?

25. Juan painted $\frac{3}{10}$ of a pole red. The rest of the pole was **not** painted. What fraction of the pole was **not** painted?

26. Find the perimeter of a square garden if each side of the garden is $\frac{3}{5}$ km long.

27. Mary cut a pizza into 16 equal slices. If she gave $\frac{3}{8}$ of the pizza to her friend, how many slices of pizza did she give away?

28. 200 children took part in a fire drill. $\frac{5}{8}$ of them were boys. How many girls were there?

29. A bucket can hold 6 liters of water. If it is $\frac{3}{4}$ full, how many liters of water does it contain?

30. Roger has $58.70. He wants to buy a radio and a watch. The watch costs $35.90 and the radio costs $28.50. How much more money does he need?

8 CONGRUENT AND SYMMETRIC FIGURES

1 Congruent Figures

When two shapes have the same size and shape, they are **congruent**.

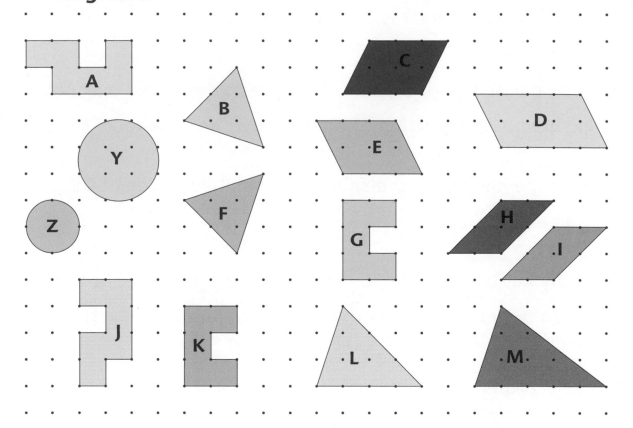

Which shapes are congruent?

When two shapes are congruent, they will fit exactly when placed on top of each other.

1. Look at each pair of shapes. Are they congruent?

(a)

(b)

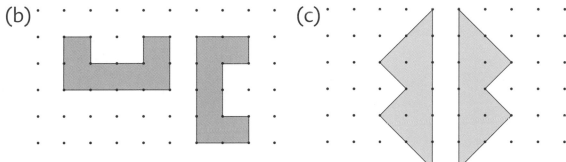

(c)

(d)

(e)

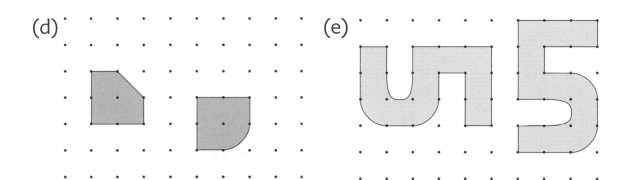

(f)

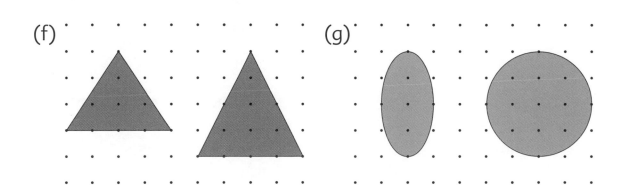

(g)

2. The two quadrilaterals, X and Y, are congruent.

(a) With which vertex of Quadrilateral X does each vertex
     of Quadrilateral Y match up?

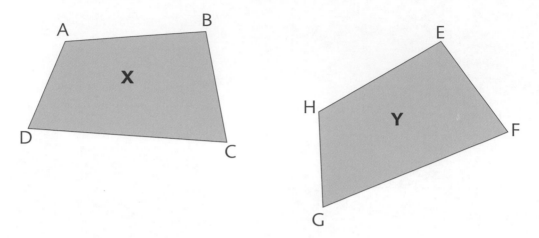

On two congruent figures, the vertices, sides and angles which fit on top of each other are called **corresponding vertices**, **corresponding sides**, and **corresponding angles**.

(b) Which side of Quadrilateral X does GH correspond to?

(c) Name another pair of corresponding sides.

Exercise 1, pages 83-85

2 Tiling Patterns

These tiling patterns are **tessellations**.
Each of them is made with congruent shapes only.

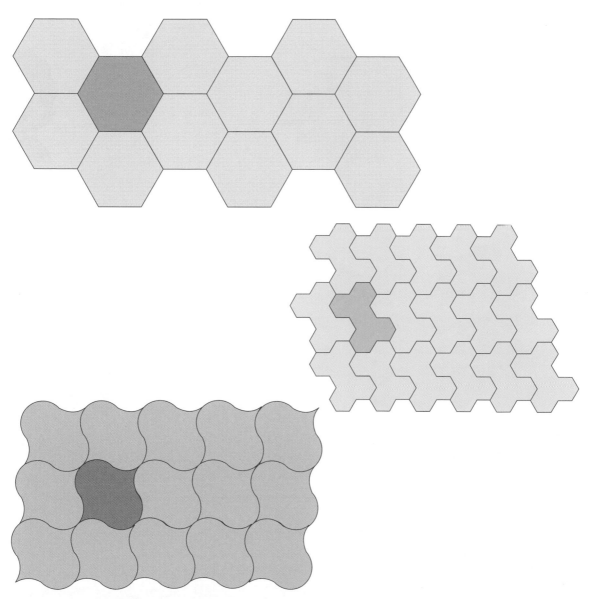

Look for some tessellations around you.

In a tessellation, the congruent shapes are fitted together with no gaps in between.

1. What shape is used in each of the following tessellations?

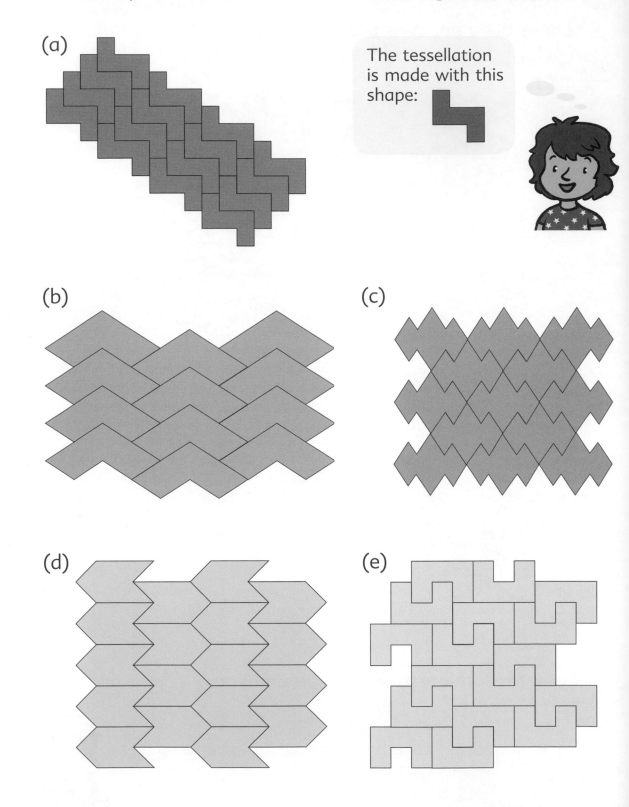

(a)

The tessellation is made with this shape:

(b)

(c)

(d)

(e)

78

Exercise 2, pages 86-88

2. A rectangle can tessellate.

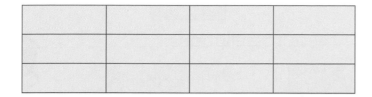

A circle cannot tessellate.

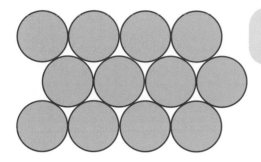

There are gaps in between the circles.

Trace and cut out each of the following shapes. Make 12 copies of each of them. Find out which shapes can tessellate.

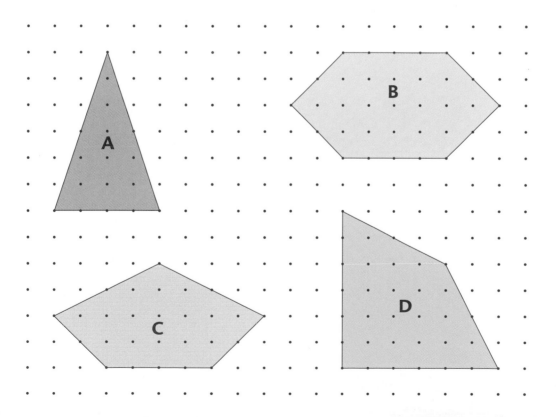

Exercise 3, pages 89-90

3. Draw and cut out many copies of this rectangle.

Use them to make these tessellations.

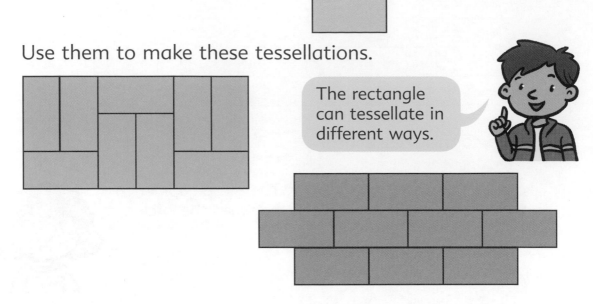

The rectangle can tessellate in different ways.

Make other tessellations with the rectangle.

4. Make as many different tessellations as you can using each of the following shapes.

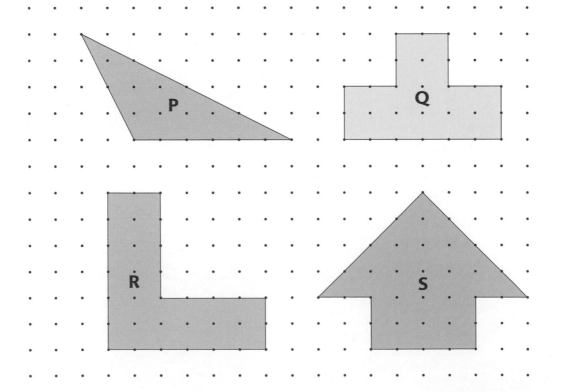

Exercise 4, pages 91-94

③ Line Symmetry

Many things around us have **symmetry**.
Here are some of them.

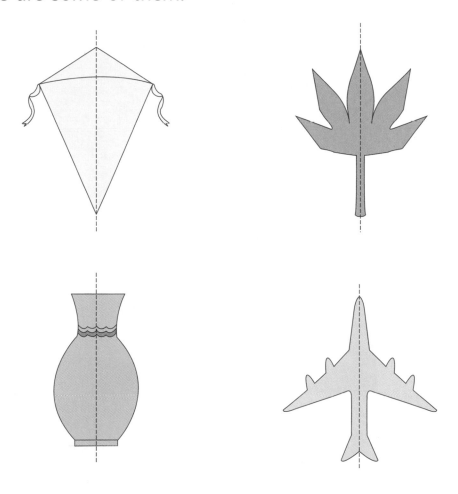

These are **symmetric figures**.
The dotted line in each figure
is a **line of symmetry**.
We say that the shape has
line symmetry.

Look for some more examples of symmetry around you.

1. Fold a piece of paper.
   Cut out a figure which starts and ends on the fold line like this.

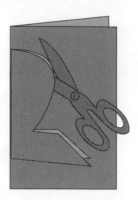

   Unfold the figure.
   You will get a symmetric figure.

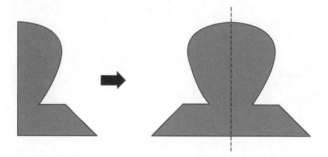

   The fold line is a line of symmetry.

2. Draw and cut out some symmetric figures.

   (a)

   (b)

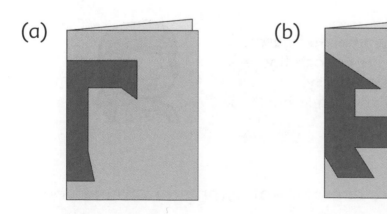

Exercise 5, pages 95-96

3. Fold each rectangle along the dotted line as shown.

(a)

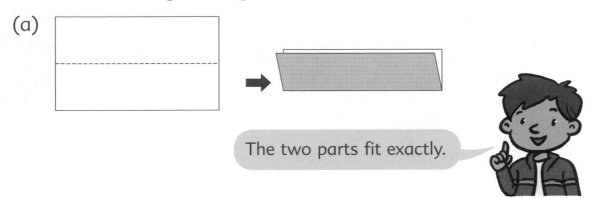

The two parts fit exactly.

The dotted line is a line of symmetry of the rectangle.

(b)

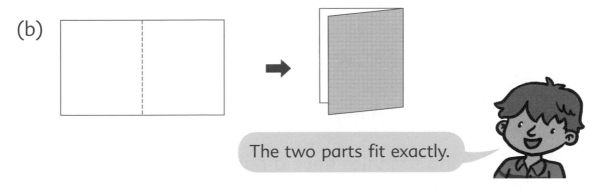

The two parts fit exactly.

The dotted line is another line of symmetry of the rectangle.

(c)

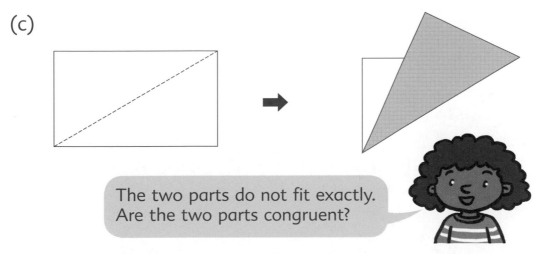

The two parts do not fit exactly.
Are the two parts congruent?

The dotted line is not a line of symmetry of the rectangle.

4. (a) An isosceles triangle has line symmetry.

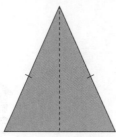

Fold along the dotted line. The two parts fit exactly.

The dotted line is a line of symmetry of the triangle.

(b) An equilateral triangle also has line symmetry.

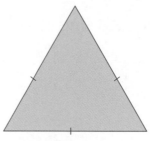

Find a line of symmetry on an equilateral triangle.

5. The following triangles have a right angle. They are called right triangles.

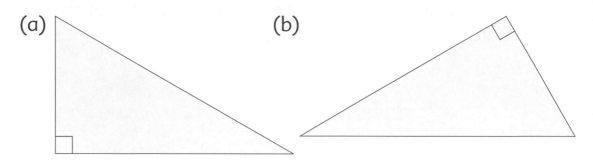

(a)

(b)

(c)

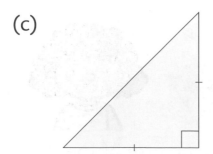

Which of these right-angled triangles has a line of symmetry?

6. Is the dotted line in each parallelogram a line of symmetry?

(a)

(b)

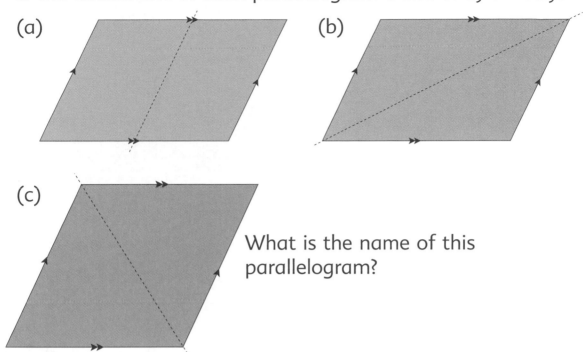

(c)

What is the name of this parallelogram?

7. Is the dotted line a line of symmetry in each trapezoid?

(a)

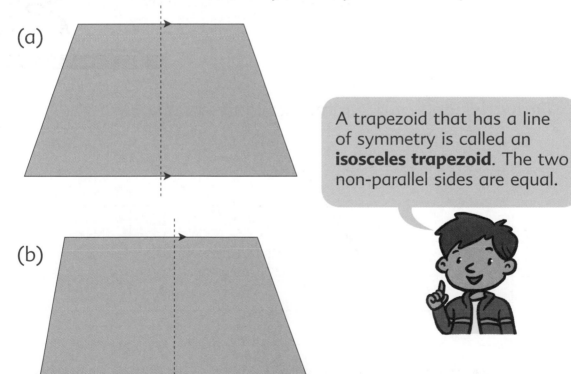

A trapezoid that has a line of symmetry is called an **isosceles trapezoid**. The two non-parallel sides are equal.

(b)

8. In each of the following figures, is the dotted line a line of symmetry?

(a)

(b)

(c)

(d)

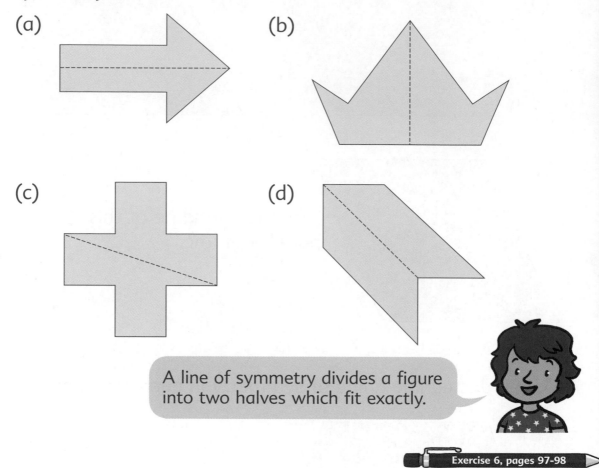

A line of symmetry divides a figure into two halves which fit exactly.

Exercise 6, pages 97-98

9. Draw this half of a symmetric figure on a square grid.

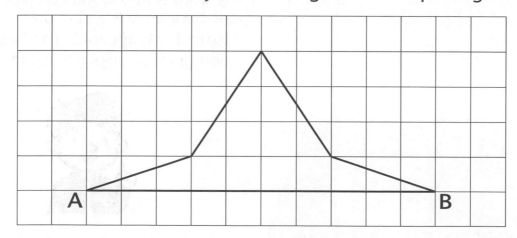

Then complete the symmetric figure with AB as a line of symmetry.

Exercise 7, pages 99-100

④ Rotational Symmetry

Trace this figure ABCD on a piece of paper. Label the vertices. Then lay it over the original figure on this page. Rotate the paper around the point O.

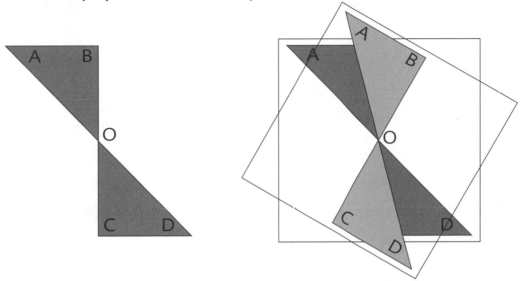

If you rotate the paper all the way so that A lies on top of A again, the two figures match.

Is there another position where the figures match before you turn the paper all the way around?

What vertex lies on top of D when the traced figure matches the original figure?

The figure has **rotational symmetry**.

> A figure has **rotational symmetry** if it can be turned around a central point and still look the same in at least one position other than the starting position.

Look for some examples of rotational symmetry around you.

1. Which of the following figures have rotational symmetry?

  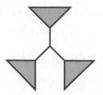 

2. This figure has rotational symmetry.
   Which line has the same length as BC?

3. Which of these quadrilaterals have rotational symmetry?

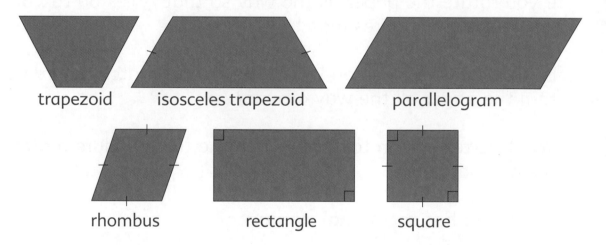

trapezoid   isosceles trapezoid   parallelogram

rhombus   rectangle   square

4. Which of these triangles have rotational symmetry?

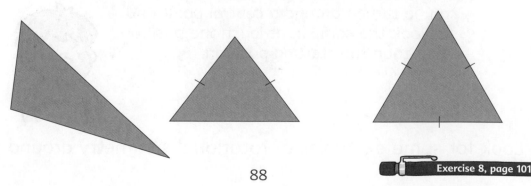

Exercise 8, page 101

REVIEW 8

1. (a) In 26,085, which digit is in the ten thousands place?
    (b) What is the value of the digit **3** in 5.23?

2. Write each of the following in figures.

    (a) ninety thousand, five hundred four
    (b) seventeen thousand, five hundred forty-one
    (c) negative four hundred five

3. Which one of the following has the digit **9** in the hundredths place?

    2.6**9**,   **9**.24,   **9**0.46,   **9**00.5

4. Write the next two numbers in each of the following regular number patterns.

    (a) 74,300, 76,300, 78,300, ,

    (b) 4.09, 4.59, 5.09, ,

    (c) 15, 10, 5, ☐, ☐

5. (a) What number is 10 more than 14,670?
    (b) What number is 1000 more than 29,083?
    (c) What number is 100 less than 10,000?
    (d) What number is 1000 less than 90,301?

6. (a) What number is 0.1 more than 6.93?
    (b) What number is 0.1 less than 5?
    (c) What number is 0.01 more than 2.4?
    (d) What number is 0.01 less than 3.612?

7. Arrange the numbers in increasing order.

   (a) 41,508, 14,058, 14,508, 41,058
   (b) 72, 24.3, 0.96, 8.54
   (c) −8, −14, −10, 15, 20

8. What is the missing number in each ?

   (a) 6.28 = 6 +   (b) 10.64 = 10.6 +

9. Find the value of each of the following expressions.

   (a) 40 × (23 − 15)   (b) 38 × 2 − 7 × 4
   (c) (36 + 24) ÷ 5   (d) 8 × (43 − 38) ÷ 2

10. Write >, < or = in place of each .

    (a) 7 × 8   9 × 7

    (b) 325 + 30   425 − 90

    (c) 45 × 10   4500 ÷ 10

    (d) 5505 − 100   5045

11. What number does each letter represent?

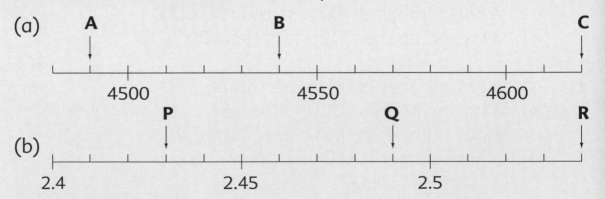

12. Round 8.45 to 1 decimal place.

13. (a) Write down two factors of 45.
    (b) Write down a common multiple of 8 and 6.

14. (a) Find the sum of 3.09, 5.92 and 1.4.
    (b) Find the product of 24 and 639.

15. Each of the following figures is made up of 6 squares.
    Which figure does **not** have a line of symmetry?
    Which figures make a cube?

16. Which of the figures have line symmetry, rotational symmetry,
    or both?

    (a)   (b)   (c)

17. The difference between two numbers is 2790. If the smaller number is 3560, what is the other number?

18. A blue ribbon is 1242 in. long. It is 9 times as long as a red ribbon. How long is the red ribbon?

19. Claire bought 6 cans of milk. Each can of milk cost $1.25. How much did Claire spend?

20. The capacity of a bottle is 1.5 qt. It is filled with 0.75 qt of water. How much more water can be poured into the bottle?

21. Carlos had $50. He spent $11.90 on a book and $27.35 on a tennis racket. How much money did he have left?

22. Sara saved $20.35. Her brother saved $16.85 more than she. How much did they save altogether?

23. Miss Bowles and 18 students went on a picnic. They spent $72 altogether. Each of the students paid $3. Miss Bowles paid the rest. How much did Miss Bowles pay?

24. Robert bought a washing machine and 3 microwave ovens for $2000. The washing machine cost $665. How much did each microwave oven cost?

25. The cost of renting a truck is $4500 a month. 4 men rented a truck for 2 months. They shared the cost equally. How much did each man pay?

9 COORDINATE GRAPHS AND CHANGES IN QUANTITIES

1 The Coordinate Grid

Who is closer to the banana, the monkey or the chimp?

We can represent the location of the animals relative to the banana with a grid.

> A **coordinate grid** has two number lines or **axes**, a **horizontal axis** and a **vertical axis**. The **origin** is 0 on both number lines.

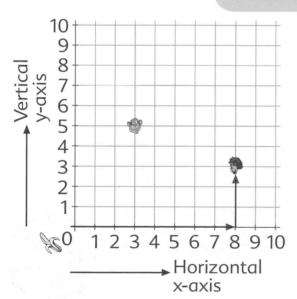

> The location of a point on the grid can be represented with a set of two distances from the origin, first the horizontal distance and then the vertical distance.

The chimp is at the position (8, 3).

→ horizontal distance

↳ vertical distance

What is the monkey's position?

93

1. **What is the position of the tree?**

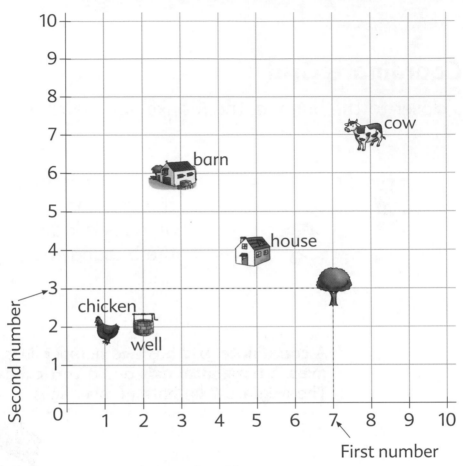

The tree is in position (7, 3).

Give the ordered pair for each of the following.
(a) house
(b) barn
(c) cow
(d) well
(e) chicken

In an **ordered pair**, the first number tells us how far to move horizontally, and the second number tells us how far to move vertically. The numbers in an ordered pair are called the **coordinates**.

2. Which point is at each of
    the following positions?

    (a) (2, 3)

    (b) (0, 9)

    (c) (5, 6)

    (d) (6, 5)

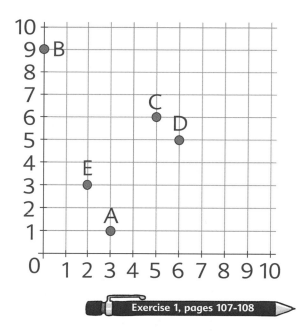

Exercise 1, pages 107-108

3. On the map, Bill's house is at (3, 3), Manuel's house is at
    (8, 3), and Tom's house is at (3, 9).

    Each square on the map is 1 unit.

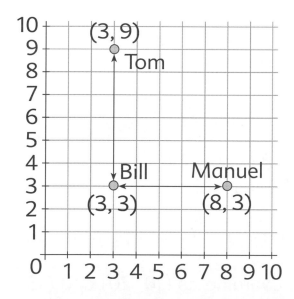

(a) What is the distance
    between Bill's house and
    Manuel's house?

(b) What is the distance
    between Bill's house and
    Tom's house?

(c) Which coordinates do
    we subtract to find the
    distance between Bill's
    house and Tom's house?

We can count the units between
the two points, or subtract the
first coordinates.

$$8 - 3 = 5$$

4. (a) Find the length of each line segment.

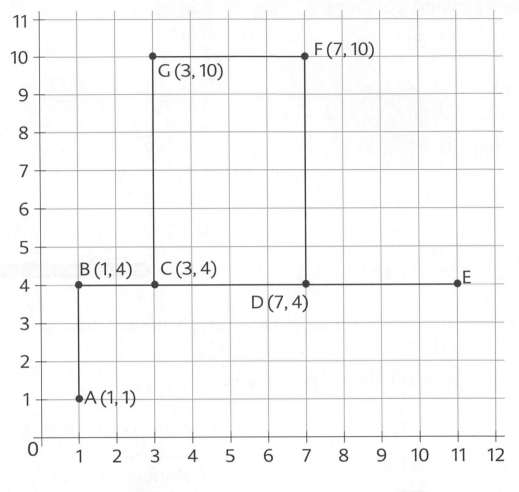

(i) AB = ▨ units   (ii) CD = ▨ units

(b) To find the length of FD, do you subtract the first or second coordinates in the ordered pairs for the points F and D?

(c) What is the distance from Point C to a point at (3, 18)?

5. Two points, P and Q, are at coordinates (10, 20) and (15, 20).
(a) How many units apart are they?
(b) To which axis is the line connecting P and Q parallel?

6. A rectangle has coordinates (2, 3), (2, 10), (6, 10), and (6, 3) on a grid with 1-cm squares. What is the perimeter of the rectangle?

96

Exercise 2, pages 109-110

❷ Changes in Quantities

Triangles, with sides measuring 1 cm, are lined up.

  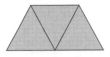 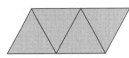

1 triangle   2 triangles   3 triangles   4 triangles

How does the perimeter change as the number of triangles changes? Complete the table.

Number of triangles	1	2	3	4	5	6
Number of 1-cm sides that form the perimeter	3	4	5	6	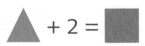	

Let  represent the number of triangles.

Let ▆ represent the number of sides.

The number of sides is ▆ more than the number of triangles.

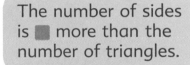

Give an equation to express the relationship between the number of triangles and the number of sides.

$$\triangle + 2 = \blacksquare$$

If ▲ is 10, what is ▆ ?

$$10 + 2 = \blacksquare$$

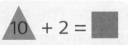

97

1. On a calendar, the number is directly below the number .

S	M	T	W	T	F	S
		1	2	3	4	5
6	7	8	9	10	11	12
13	14	15				

(a) Complete the table.

●	1	2	3	4	5	6	7
◆							

(b) Complete the equation to show the relationship between
◆ and ●.

◆ = ● + ?

(c) What is ◆ if ● = 15?

2. The area of a square is given by the formula

$A = s \times s$

where A stands for the area and s stands for the length of the side.

(a) Complete the table to show what happens to the area if the side increases by 1 unit.

s	1	2	3	4	5	6
A						

(b) What is A if $s = 24$?

98

3. The length of a rectangle is 3 times the width.
   (a) If *l* stands for the length of the rectangle and *w* stands for the width of the rectangle, give a formula for the length of the rectangle.

   $l = \boxed{}$

   (b) If the width of the rectangle is 4 cm, what is the length?
   (c) If the width of the rectangle is 8 cm, what is the perimeter?
   (d) If the width of the rectangle is 10 cm, what is the area?

4. Mrs. Murphy wants to buy a skirt and some shirts.
   The skirt costs $20.
   Each shirt costs $5.

   (a) Complete the table to show how much money she must spend if she wants to buy more than one shirt.

Number of shirts	1	2	3	4	5	s
Cost of shirts in dollars	5	10	▢	▢	▢	5 × s
Cost of 1 skirt in dollars	20	20	20	20	▢	20
Total cost	▢	▢	▢	▢	▢	(5 × s) + 20

   Let *C* represent the total cost.

   $C = (5 \times s) + 20$

   (b) What is the value of *C* if *s* = 6?
   (c) Mrs. Murphy has $47.
       She wants to buy a skirt and some shirts.
       How many shirts can she buy?

Exercise 3, pages 111-112

3 Graphing Changes in Quantities

The length, *l*, of a rectangle is 2 cm more than the width, *w*.

$$l = w + 2$$

w	l	(w, l)
1	3	(1, 3)
2	4	(2, 4)
3	5	(3, 5)
4	6	(4, 6)

We can write the width and the length as an ordered pair, and show the values on a coordinate grid.

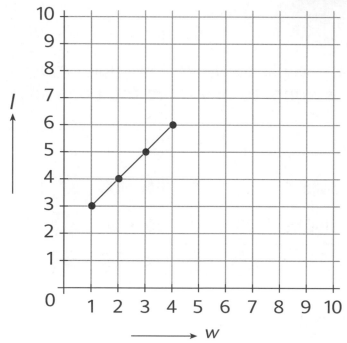

When the points are connected, we get a straight line.

How can we use the grid to find the length of the rectangle if the width is 6 cm?

1. This graph shows the relationship between two numbers, x and y.

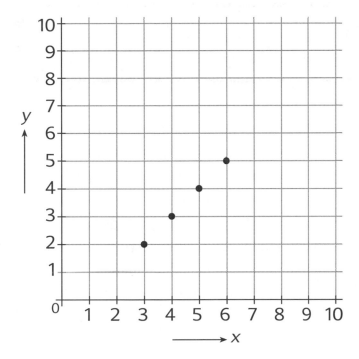

(a) Use a ruler to find the value of y when x is 8.
(b) What is the value of x when y is 6?
(c) What is the value of x when y is 0?
(d) Complete the table.

x	2	3	4	5	6	7
y						

(e) Give an equation that shows the relationship between x and y.

$y =$

Exercise 4, pages 113-114

REVIEW 9

1.

251.83   132.85

123.58   135.28

(a) Write the numbers in increasing order.
(b) What is the value of the digit 2 in each number?
(c) In which number does the digit 5 stand for 5 tenths?

2. (a) In 5630, which digit is in the **hundreds** place?
   (b) In 12.78, which digit is in the **tenths** place?

3. A hotel has 64 floors above the ground and 3 floors below ground. The floors are labeled according to their distance from ground level. The third floor above ground level is called Level 3. What would the third level below ground be called?

4. Write each of the following as a decimal.

   (a) $400 + 50 + 0.07$ (b) $30 + 5 + \frac{3}{10} + \frac{3}{100}$

   (c) $30 + 0.5 + 0.04$ (d) $100 + 7 + 0.08$

5. Estimate and then multiply.
   (a) 456×60 (b) 306×27 (c) 783×41

6. Find the value of each of the following.

   (a) $\frac{2}{3} + \frac{7}{9}$ (b) $2 - \frac{5}{8}$ (c) $\frac{4}{5} + \frac{3}{5}$

   (d) $\frac{7}{8} - \frac{3}{4}$ (e) $\frac{5}{6}$ of 60   (f) $\frac{3}{4}$ of 200

7. (a) Express 1.36 as a fraction in its simplest form.

   (b) Express $3\frac{11}{50}$ as a decimal.

8. This table shows the amount of money Susan spent in 5 days.

Monday	Tuesday	Wednesday	Thursday	Friday
$3.45	$2.05	$2	$3.60	$1.15

Find the total amount of money she spent in 5 days.

9. Find the perimeter and area of each figure. (All lines meet at right angles.)

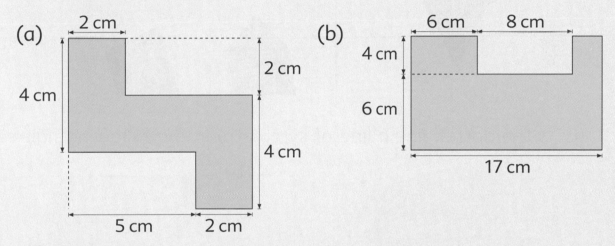

(a)

(b)

10. The perimeter of a rectangle is 42 in. If the length of the rectangle is 12 in., find its width.

11. The area of a square flower bed is 25 m². Find its perimeter.

12. (a) A shop is open from 11:25 a.m. to 7 p.m. How long is the shop open for?

    (b) A movie started at 7:50 p.m. It lasted 2 hours 15 minutes. When did the movie end?

13. Does a circle have rotational symmetry?

103

14. Write a single expression to show that a number represented by p is added to a number represented by q, and then the sum is divided by a number represented by r.

15. Which solid can be formed by the given net?

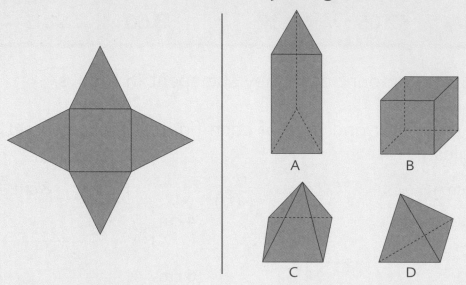

16. Is the dotted line a line of symmetry in the following figures?

(a)

(b)

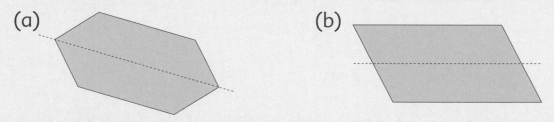

17. After spending $\frac{3}{5}$ of his money on a tennis racket, Shawn had $14 left. How much did the tennis racket cost?

18. Terry had $34. He spent $\frac{2}{5}$ of the money on a picture book. Then he spent $8.25 on a birthday present. How much money did he spend altogether?

19. Gabrielle bought a roll of ribbon to decorate 6 presents. She used 1.28 yd of ribbon for each present. If she had 2.32 yd of ribbon left, how many yards of ribbon did she buy?

20.

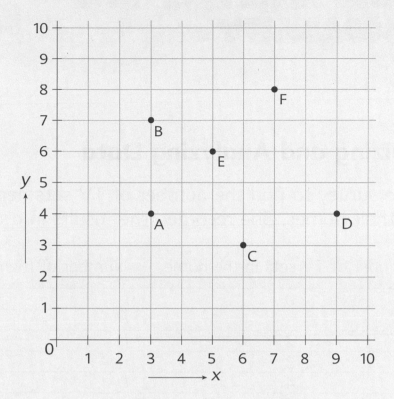

(a) What is the ordered pair for Point C?

(b) What point is at (7, 8)?

(c) What is the distance between the points A and D in units?

(d) Which coordinates, the first or second, of the ordered pair do you subtract to find the distance from A to B?

(e) Point Z is at (5, 12). How far is it from Point E?

(f) Another point that would be on a line formed by the points A, E, and F is (9,   ).

(g) Fill in the table for the ordered pair (x, y) corresponding to the points A, E and F.

	A	E	F
x			
y			

(h) Write an equation showing the relationship between x and y for the points on a line through the points A and F.

1 Organizing and Analyzing Data

Lila did a survey to find the number of TV sets her friends have in their homes. She recorded the results in a tally chart.

Number of TV sets in the home	Number of friends
0	/
1	/
2	//
3	//
4	////
5	/

How can Lila organize the data?

The data can be organized from the **least** to the **most**.

0, 1, 2, 2, 3, 3, 4, 4, 4, 4, 5

(a) What is the lowest number of TV sets?
(b) What is the highest number of TV sets?
(c) What is the middle number of the set of data?

0, 1, 2, 2, 3,③, 4, 4, 4, 4, 5

To find the middle number, mark off pairs of data starting at the ends.

The middle number of a set of data is called the **median**.

Half of her friends have at most 3 TV sets and half of her friends have at least 3 TV sets.

106

The data can also be recorded and shown on a **line plot**.

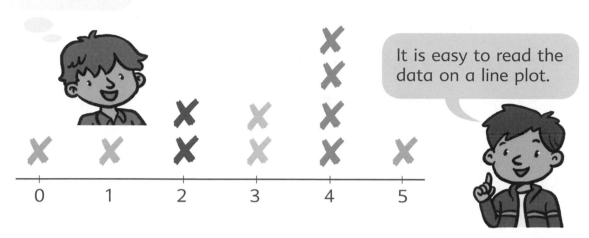

It is easy to read the data on a line plot.

To find the median on a line plot, mark off pairs of crosses starting at the ends from the bottom up.

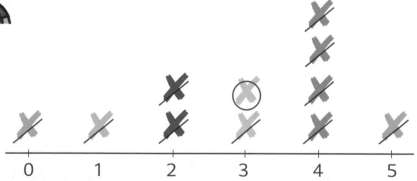

1. Sam had the following scores for his last seven mathematics tests.

    85, 77, 83, 95, 86, 77, 90

    (a) Organize Sam's test scores from the lowest to the highest.

    77, 77,

    (b) What is Sam's highest score?
    (c) What is his lowest score?
    (d) What is his median score?

2. Gayle surveyed her friends to find the number of hours they spend exercising each week. She recorded the data using a line plot.

    What is the median number of hours her friends exercise each week?

    If there are 2 numbers in the middle that are equal, then that value is the median.

3. John weighed the dogs at the veterinarian's clinic and recorded the data in the table below.

Weight in lb	40	35	46	54	22	61	32	45	67	50

(a) Organize the data beginning with the smallest.
(b) What is the median weight of the dogs?

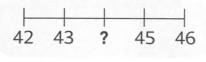

42   43   ?   45   46

If there are 2 numbers in the middle that are different, the number that is halfway between them is the median.

Exercise 1, pages 121-123

4. Sarah surveyed her friends to find out which color they like the most and recorded the results on a tally chart.

Colour	Number of friends
Red	TTHL I
Green	TTHL IIII
Blue	TTHL

(a) Which color do her friends like the most?

(b) What color do her friends like the least?

I think I will wear a green dress for my birthday party.

The value that appears most often in a set of data is called the **mode**.

5. Timothy asked his classmates which kind of pets they like the most and recorded the data in a bar graph.

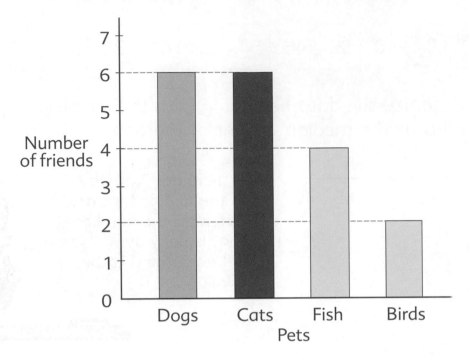

(a) Timothy surveyed  students.

(b)  more friends like dogs than birds.

(c) 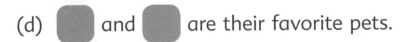 fewer friends like fish than cats.

(d)  and ___ are their favorite pets.

(e) ___ are their least favorite pet.

There can be more than one mode.

6. Josh asked some of his friends their ages and recorded the data in a line plot.

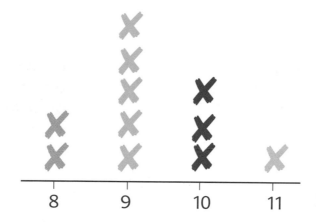

(a) Josh surveyed ⬜ friends.

(b) His two youngest friends are both ⬜ years old.

(c) His oldest friend is ⬜ years old.

(d) The age difference between his oldest and youngest friends is ⬜ years.

(e) The median age of his friends is ⬜ years.

(f) More of his friends are ⬜ years old.

(g) The mode of the data is ⬜ years.

Exercise 2, page 124

② Probability Experiments

Mary and Sam wanted to conduct a coin tossing experiment.

I think we will get more tails than heads.

Mary

I think we will get the same number of heads and tails.

Sam

They took turns tossing the coin and recorded their results in a tally chart.

Heads	~~HHHH~~ I
Tails	IIII

They got heads out of 10 times.

6 out of 10 = $\frac{6}{10}$

$\frac{6}{10} = \frac{3}{5}$

We got heads $\frac{3}{5}$ of the time.

1. Sam rolled a regular six-sided die several times. He recorded the results on the line plot below.

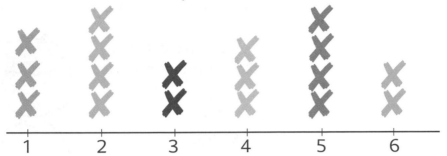

(a) Sam rolled the die ⬜ times.

(b) He rolled a two ⬜ out of ⬜ times.

(c) He rolled a two $\dfrac{4}{18} = \dfrac{\square}{9}$ of the time.

(d) He rolled a four ⬜ out of ⬜ times.

(e) He rolled a four $\dfrac{3}{\square} = \dfrac{1}{\square}$ of the time.

(f) He rolled a six $\dfrac{\square}{\square} = \dfrac{\square}{\square}$ of the time.

(g) He rolled an odd number $\dfrac{\square}{\square} = \dfrac{\square}{\square}$ of the time.

(h) He rolled a number smaller than five $\dfrac{\square}{\square}$ of the time.

2. Lili tossed a coin 20 times and got 8 heads and 12 tails.

(a) Lili got heads ⬜ out of ⬜ times.

(b) What fraction of the coin tosses were heads?

(c) Lili got tails ⬜ out of ⬜ times.

(d) What fraction of the coin tosses were tails?

113

Exercise 3, pages 125–126

③ Order of Outcomes

Patti tosses a coin 3 times. In what different ways might she get heads and tails?

I will make a tree diagram to find out.

Let H stand for heads and T stand for tails.

First toss	Second toss	Third toss	Outcomes
H	H	H	heads, heads, heads
		T	heads, heads, tails
	T	H	heads, tails, heads
		T	heads, tails, tails
T	H	H	tails, heads, heads
		T	tails, heads, tails
	T	H	tails, tails, heads
		T	tails, tails, tails

If I get heads first?

If I get tails first?

We call all the different ways **possible outcomes**.

There are ⬜ possible outcomes.

1. Sam spins a spinner twice. Complete the tree diagram to find the possible outcomes.

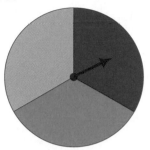

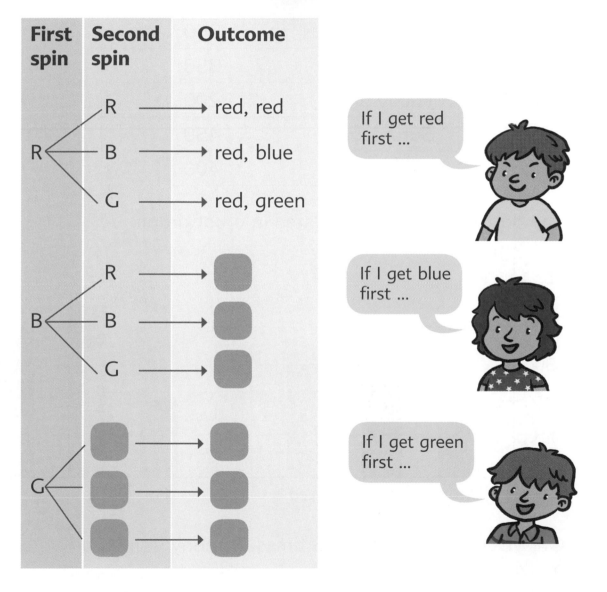

First spin	Second spin	Outcome
R	R	red, red
	B	red, blue
	G	red, green
B	R	
	B	
	G	
G		

If I get red first …

If I get blue first …

If I get green first …

There are ⬜ possible outcomes.

Exercise 4, pages 127-128

④ Bar Graphs

This table shows the number of people who visited an art exhibition during a week.

Day	Number of visitors
Monday	150
Tuesday	250
Wednesday	300
Thursday	350
Friday	200
Saturday	450
Sunday	400

The data can also be presented in a bar graph.

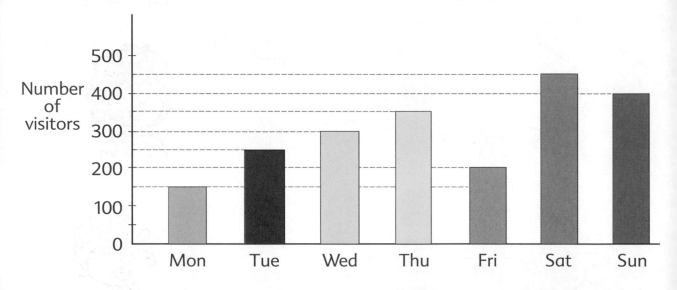

On which day were there 3 times as many visitors as on Monday?

For how many days were there at least twice as many visitors as on Monday?

1. The bar graph shows how a group of children travel to school. Use the graph to answer the questions which follow.

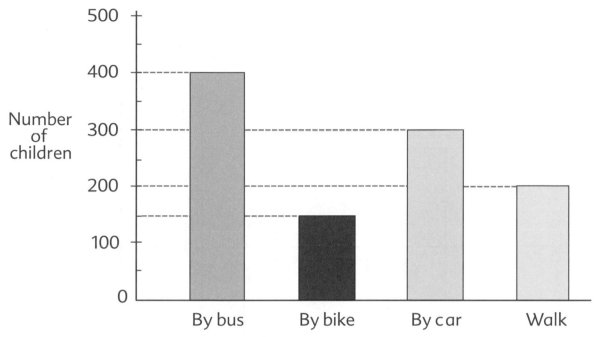

(a) How many children travel to school by bike?
(b) How many more children travel to school by bus than by bike?
(c) How many children are there in the group?
(d) What fraction of the group of children walk to school?

2. The bar graph shows the number of girls and boys in four groups A, B, C and D. Use the graph to answer the questions which follow.

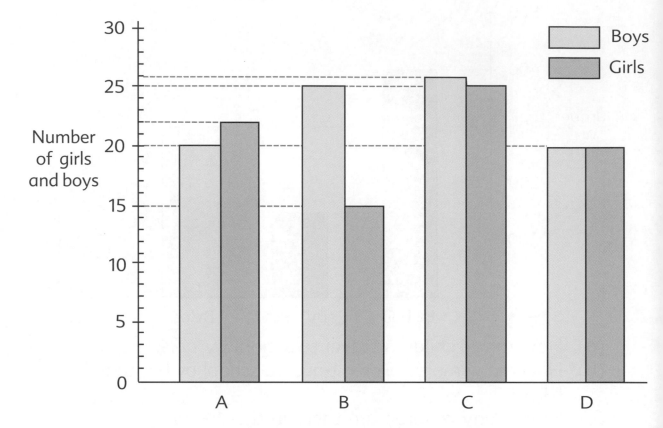

(a) Which groups have more boys than girls?
(b) Which group has the same number of boys as girls?
(c) What is the total number of children in Group A?
(d) How many children are there altogether?

Exercise 5, pages 129-130

⑤ Line Graphs

This table shows the attendance at a swimming pool across 5 months.

Month	August	September	October	November	December
Number of people	2500	3500	2000	2500	4000

The data can also be presented in a **line graph**.

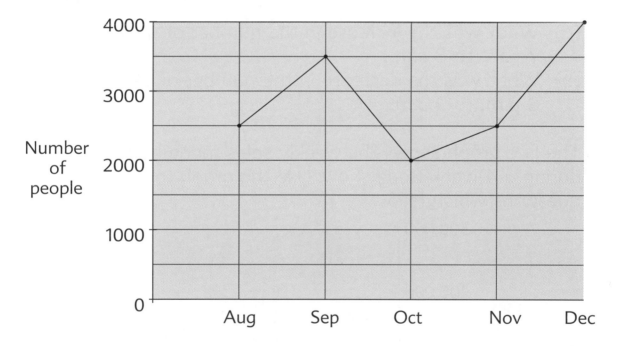

(a) There was an increase in attendance from August to September. What was the increase?

(b) There was a decrease in attendance from September to October. What was the decrease?

(c) What was the difference between the attendance in September and the attendance in December?

1. The line graph shows the number of people in a supermarket by the hour from 5 p.m. to 10 p.m. Use the graph to answer the questions which follow.

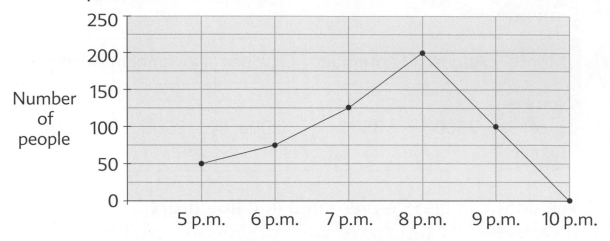

(a) What was the increase in the number of people from 7 p.m. to 8 p.m.?

(b) What was the decrease in the number of people from 8 p.m. to 9 p.m.?

2. The line graph shows the weekly sales made by a company during a 4-week trade show. Use the graph to answer the questions which follow.

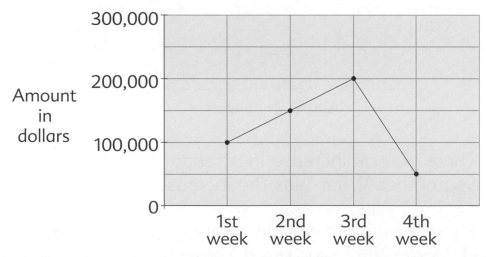

(a) What was the increase in sales from the 1st week to the 3rd week?

(b) What was the decrease in sales from the 3rd week to the 4th week?

Exercise 6, pages 131-134

3. This line graph shows the exchange rate between U.S. dollars and Singapore dollars some years ago.

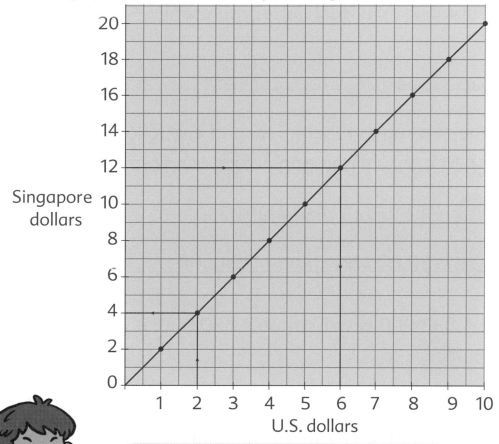

Singapore dollars

U.S. dollars

2 U.S. dollars can be exchanged for 4 Singapore dollars. 12 Singapore dollars can be exchanged for 6 U.S. dollars.

(a) How many Singapore dollars can be exchanged for 9 U.S. dollars?

(b) How many U.S. dollars can be exchanged for 10 Singapore dollars?

(c) How many U.S. dollars can be exchanged for 16 Singapore dollars?

(d) Use s to stand for Singapore dollars and u to stand for U.S. dollars. Write a formula to show the relationship between U.S. and Singapore dollars. u =

(e) How many Singapore dollars can be exchanged for 30 U.S. dollars?

Exercise 7, pages 135-136

REVIEW 10

1. What number does each letter represent?

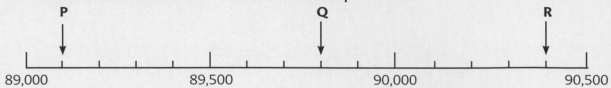

2. Give the missing number in each of the following.

    (a) 3,649,500 = 3,000,000 + ⬜ + 40,000 + 9500

    (b) ⬜ is 100 more than 4,991,200.

    (c) ⬜ is 10,000 less than 6,304,500.

3. When 4,832,900 is written as 4,830,000, it is rounded to the nearest ⬜ .

4. (a) What number is 2 less than −10?
   (b) What number is 2 more than −10?

5. Write a positive or negative number to represent each situation.

   (a) 15 feet underground   (b) 9 seconds before liftoff
   (c) a gain of 5 pounds   (d) 40 degrees above freezing
   (e) 12 meters below sea level

6. Mrs. Cohen bought a dress which cost about $23.
   Which of the following could be the actual cost of the dress?

       $22.10, $23.95, $22.50, $23.50

7. In 8.6**2**, the value of the digit **2** is ⬜ .

8. In 62.85, which digit is in the **hundredths** place?

9. Write the missing number in each of the following.

 (a) [ ] is 0.01 more than 20.99.

 (b) [ ] is 0.01 less than 48.03.

 (c) $1.06 = 1 +$ [ ]

 (d) $2.28 = 2 +$ [ ] $+ 0.08$

10. Write $10 + \dfrac{3}{100}$ as a decimal.

11. Arrange the numbers in increasing order.

 40.62,   40.26,   42.06,   42.6

12. What number must be added to 7.25 to give the answer 11?

13. Find the sum of 45.96 and 68.2.

14. Find the difference between 30.05 and 9.2.

15. Find the product of 14 and 35.

16. For each of the following, estimate the product. Then multiply.

 (a) 3.7×4 (b) 6.6×58 (c) 2.85×49

17. Divide. Round the answers to 1 decimal place.

 (a) $7 \div 6$ (b) $24.8 \div 7$ (c) $21.5 \div 8$

18. What fraction of
 the figure is shaded?

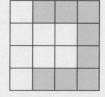

19. Write $\dfrac{24}{15}$ in its simplest form.

20. Mary, Susan, and Ken shared a pizza. Mary and Susan each had $\frac{3}{8}$ of the pizza. What fraction of the pizza did Ken have?

21. There were 120 people at a concert. $\frac{2}{3}$ of them were adults. How many children were there?

22. There were some marbles in a bag. $\frac{1}{3}$ of them were red, $\frac{1}{6}$ of them were blue, and the rest were yellow.
    (a) What fraction of the marbles were yellow?
    (b) If there were 15 yellow marbles, how many marbles were there altogether?

23. Sharon saved $10.50 in 3 weeks. If she saves the same amount each week, how much will she save in 9 weeks?

24. The area of a square is 64 in.^{2}
    (a) Find the length of one side of the square.
    (b) Find the perimeter of the square.

25. Find the area of the figure.
    (All lines meet at right angles.)

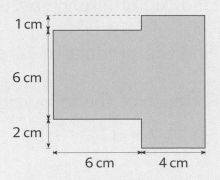

26. How many right angles are equal to $\frac{1}{2}$ a complete turn?

27. Measure ∠x and ∠y.

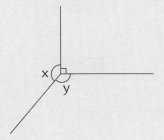

28. Mark a right angle (⌐) to show a pair of perpendicular lines. Draw arrowheads (⟋) to show a pair of parallel lines.

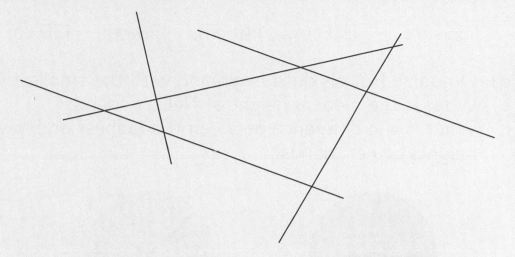

29.

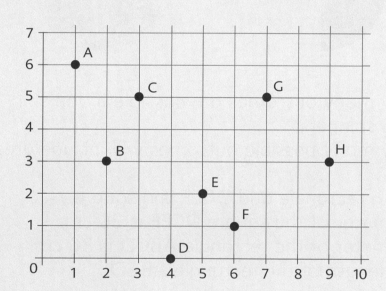

(a) Point D is at ⬛.

(b) Point G is at ⬛.

(c) Point ⬛ is at (6, 1).

(d) Point ⬛ is at (9, 3).

30. Nellie measured her friends' heights.
The heights are listed below.

135 cm,   130 cm,   140 cm,   128 cm,   130 cm

(a) Organize Nellie's data beginning with the smallest.
(b) What is the median height of Nellie's friends?
(c) What is the difference between the highest and lowest
heights of her friends?

31.

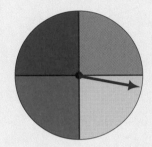 

(a) How many outcomes are possible if you spin
both spinners?
(b) How many possible outcomes will include green?

32. ABCD is a rectangle and DCEF is a square.
The perimeter of the square DCEF is 20 cm.
The perimeter of the rectangle ABCD is 36 cm.
Find the length of the rectangle ABCD.

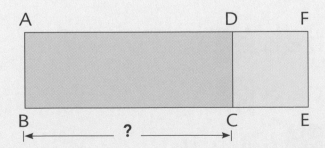

33. The graph shows the number of cars Mr. Shaw sold in the first six months of a year.

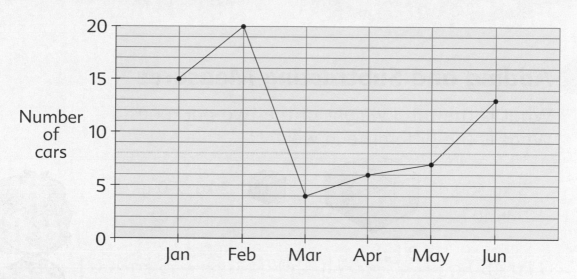

(a) What was the decrease in the number of cars sold between February and March?

(b) What was the total number of cars sold in the six months?

(c) Mr. Shaw received a commission of $1000 for every car he sold. How much commission did he receive in February?

11 MEASURES AND VOLUME

1 Adding and Subtracting Measures

What is the total weight of the two packages?
What is the difference in weight?

3 kg 450 g  2 kg 650 g
7 lb 10 oz   5 lb 14 oz

$$3 \text{ kg } 450 \text{ g} \xrightarrow{+ 2 \text{ kg}} 5 \text{ kg } 450 \text{ g} \xrightarrow{+ 650 \text{ g}} 6 \text{ kg } 100 \text{ g}$$

> 1100 g = 1 kg 100 g

$$3 \text{ kg } 450 \text{ g} \xrightarrow{- 2 \text{ kg}} 1 \text{ kg } 450 \text{ g} \xrightarrow{- 650 \text{ g}} 800 \text{ g}$$

> 1 kg − 650 g = 350 g
> 350 g + 450 g = 800 g

$$7 \text{ lb } 10 \text{ oz} \xrightarrow{+ 5 \text{ lb}} 12 \text{ lb } 10 \text{ oz} \xrightarrow{+ 14 \text{ oz}} 13 \text{ lb } 8 \text{ oz}$$

> 24 oz = 1 lb 8 oz

$$7 \text{ lb } 10 \text{ oz} \xrightarrow{- 5 \text{ lb}} 2 \text{ lb } 10 \text{ oz} \xrightarrow{- 14 \text{ oz}} 1 \text{ lb } 12 \text{ oz}$$

> 1 lb − 14 oz = 2 oz

Conversion of Measurements

Length
1 m = 100 cm   1 yd = 3 ft
1 km = 1000 m   1 ft = 12 in.

Weight
1 kg = 1000 g   1 lb = 16 oz

Capacity
1 ℓ = 1000 ml   1 gal = 4 qt
                        1 qt = 2 pt
                        1 pt = 2 c

Time
1 year = 12 months
1 week = 7 days
1 day   = 24 hours
1 hour = 60 minutes
1 minute = 60 seconds

1. Find the missing numbers.

   (a) 4 ft = ⬜ in.

   (b) 9 m = ⬜ cm

   (c) 8 days = ⬜ hours

   (d) 12 lb = ⬜ oz

   1 ft = 12 in.
   4 ft = 4 × 12 in.
       = ⬜

2. Find the missing numbers.

   (a) 4 ℓ 250 ml = ⬜ ml

   (b) 5 km 40 m = ⬜ m

   (c) 4 years 5 months = ⬜ months

   (d) 1 hour 20 minutes = ⬜ minutes

   4 ℓ = 4000 ml
   4000 ml + 250 ml = ⬜

3. Find the missing numbers.

   (a) 8 ft = ⬜ yd ⬜ ft

   (b) 602 cm = ⬜ m ⬜ cm

   (c) 2400 g = ⬜ kg ⬜ g

   8 ft
   ╱ ╲
   6 ft   2 ft
   6 ft = 2 yd

4. Subtract.

    (a) 1 kg − 550 g   (b) 1 ft − 7 in.

    (c) 1 h − 20 min   (d) 1 lb − 11 oz

5. Add or subtract in compound units.

    (a) 20 ft 9 in. + 16 ft 10 in. = ⬜ ft ⬜ in.

    (b) 40 kg 20 g − 5 kg 400 g = ⬜ kg ⬜ g

    (c) 5 min 20 s + 6 min 40 s = ⬜ min ⬜ s

    (d) 13 gal 1 qt − 4 gal 3 qt = ⬜ gal ⬜ qt

6. The total weight of two watermelons is 20 lb. The larger
    watermelon weighs 13 lb 9 oz. What is the weight of the
    smaller watermelon?

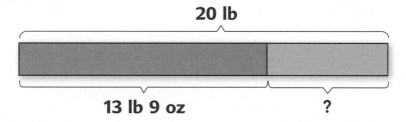

20 lb

13 lb 9 oz   **?**

7. Three beakers contain 1 ℓ 450 ml, 650 ml, and 1 ℓ 20 ml of
    solution respectively.
    What is the total amount of solution in the three beakers?

Exercise 1, pages 144-145

❷ Multiplying Measures

The 3 packages are of the same weight.
Each of them weighs 1 kg 200 g.
What is the total weight of the 3 packages?

1 kg 200 g × 3 = ⬜ kg ⬜ g

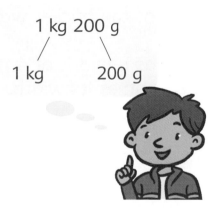

The total weight of the 3 packages is ⬜ kg ⬜ g.

1. The distance around a track was 1 km 300 m. Alex ran round the track 4 times. How far did he run?

   1 km 300 m × 4 = ⬜ km ⬜ m

   He ran ⬜ km ⬜ m.

2. Gerald filled a tank completely with 4 buckets of water. Each bucket contained 2 gal 3 qt of water. What was the capacity of the tank?

   2 gal 3 qt × 4 = ⬜ gal ⬜ qt

   = ⬜ gal

   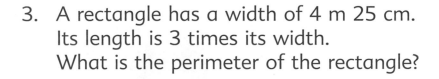

   The capacity of the bucket was ⬜ gal.

3. A rectangle has a width of 4 m 25 cm.
   Its length is 3 times its width.
   What is the perimeter of the rectangle?

   Length = 4 m 25 cm × 3

   = ⬜ m ⬜ cm

   Perimeter = 2 × (width + length)

   = 2 × (4 m 25 cm + ⬜)

   = 2 × ⬜

   = ⬜

③ Dividing Measures

Jane cut a ribbon 5 m 20 cm long into 4 equal pieces to make flowers. What was the length of each piece?

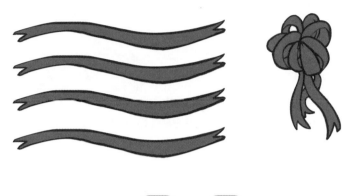

5 m 20 cm ÷ 4 = ⬜ m ⬜ cm

5 m 20 cm
／　　　＼
4 m　　　120 cm

The length of each piece was ⬜ m ⬜ cm.

1. If the total weight of 5 bags of flour is 5 kg 650 g, find the weight of each bag of flour.

    5 kg 650 g ÷ 5 = ⬜ kg ⬜ g

    The weight of each bag of flour is ⬜ kg ⬜ g.

2. A tailor took 7 hours 30 minutes to sew 6 shirts. How long did he take to sew one shirt?

    7 h 30 min = 6 h 90 min

    7 h 30 min ÷ 6 = ⬜ h ⬜ min

    He took ⬜ h ⬜ min to sew one shirt.

3. Marina poured 3 ℓ 200 ml of milk equally into 8 glasses. How many milliliters of milk were there in each glass?

    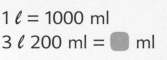
    1 ℓ = 1000 ml
    3 ℓ 200 ml = ⬜ ml

    3 ℓ 200 ml ÷ 8 = ⬜ ml

    There were ⬜ ml of milk in each glass.

Exercise 3, pages 148-149

PRACTICE A

1. Multiply in compound units.

   (a) 3 km 200 m × 5   (b) 4 ℓ 300 ml × 4
   (c) 2 h 20 min × 5   (d) 5 kg 200 g × 3
   (e) 6 m 20 cm × 6   (f) 3 yd 2 ft × 7

2. Divide in compound units.

   (a) 2 ℓ 240 ml ÷ 2   (b) 5 km 300 m ÷ 2
   (c) 1 h 30 min ÷ 5   (d) 4 kg 500 g ÷ 3
   (e) 2 m 60 cm ÷ 4   (f) 4 ft 3 in. ÷ 3

3. Mrs. Gray used 2 bottles of syrup to make drinks. Each bottle contained 1 ℓ 275 ml of syrup. How much syrup did she use?

4. Kent bought 3 kg 570 g of beans. He packed them equally into 3 bags. What was the weight of the beans in each bag?

5. Henry spent 3 hours 30 minutes every morning painting his house. He finished painting his whole house in 5 mornings. How much time did he spend painting his whole house?

6. A pineapple weighs 1 kg 800 g. A watermelon is 3 times as heavy as the pineapple.
   (a) What is the weight of the watermelon?
   (b) What is the total weight of the two fruits?

7. Maureen works 8 hours 30 minutes every day in a factory. She is paid $5 each hour.
   (a) How many hours does she work in 6 days?
   (b) How much does she earn in 6 days?

8. A rope 3 m 66 cm long was cut into two pieces. The longer piece was twice as long as the shorter piece. What was the length of the longer piece?

9. Hillary used 2 bags of sugar to make 8 cakes. One bag contained 1 kg 240 g of sugar and the other contained 1 kg 160 g of sugar. If she used the same amount of sugar for each cake, how much sugar did she use for each cake?

10. A meter of ribbon cost $4. Mary bought 2 ribbons each of length 3 m 50 cm. How much did she pay for the 2 pieces of ribbon?

④ Cubic Units

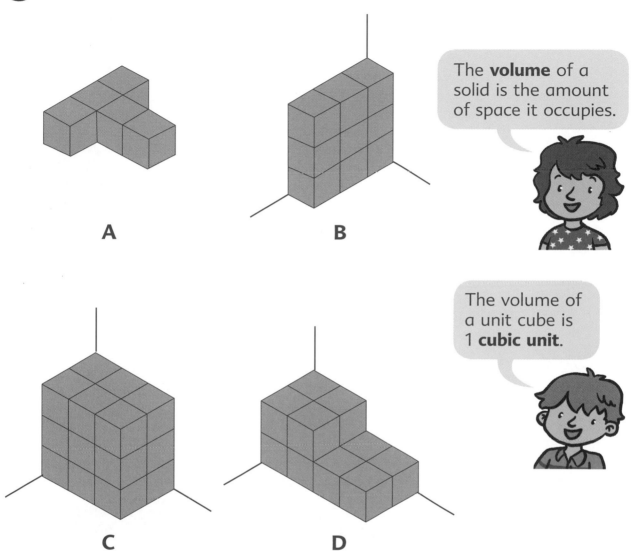

A

B

C

D

The **volume** of a solid is the amount of space it occupies.

The volume of a unit cube is 1 **cubic unit**.

These solids are built using unit cubes.
What is the volume of each of the solids?
Which solid has the greatest volume?

1. The figure shows a 1-cm cube.
   Each edge of the cube is 1 cm long.
   The volume of the cube is 1 **cubic centimeter (cm³)**.

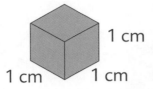

The cubic centimeter is a unit of volume. We write **cm³** for cubic centimeter.

Use two 1-cm cubes to build this solid.

The volume of the solid is 2 cm³.

Add another 1-cm cube to build this solid.

The volume of the solid is ⬜ cm³.

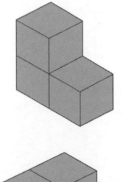

How many 1-cm cubes are needed to build this solid?

The volume of the solid is ⬜ cm³.

2. The rectangular prism is made up of 1-cm cubes. Find its volume.

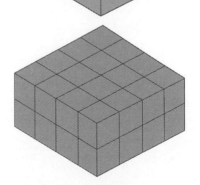

138

3. The following solids are made up of 1-cm cubes. Find the volume of each solid.

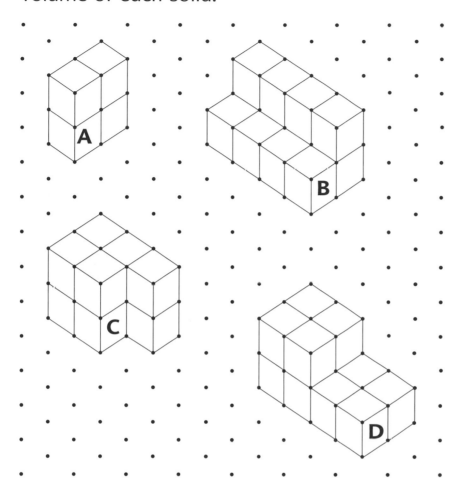

Exercise 4, page 150

⑤ Volume of Rectangular Prisms

The rectangular prism is made up of 1-cm cubes.

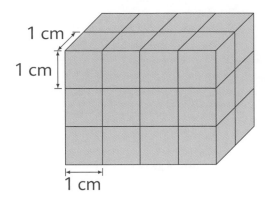

4 × 2 = 8
There are 8 cubes in each layer.

8 × 3 = 24
There are 24 cubes altogether.

The length of the rectangular prism is 4 cm.

Its width is 2 cm.

4 × 2 × 3

Its height is 3 cm.

Its volume is ⬜ cm³.

The rectangular prism measures 4 cm by 2 cm by 3 cm.

1 cm

1 cm

1 cm

3 cm

2 cm

4 cm

Volume of rectangular prism = Length × Width × Height

1. The following rectangular prisms are made up of 1-cm cubes. Find the length, width, height, and volume of each rectangular prism.

(a)

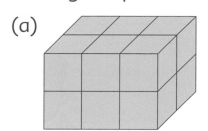

Length = ⬜ cm

Width = ⬜ cm

Height = ⬜ cm

Volume = ⬜ cm³

(b)

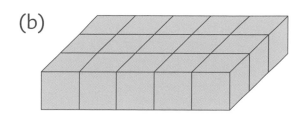

Length = ⬜ cm

Width = ⬜ cm

Height = ⬜ cm

Volume = ⬜ cm³

(c)

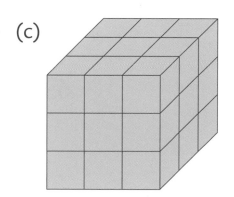

Length = ⬜ cm

Width = ⬜ cm

Height = ⬜ cm

Volume = ⬜ cm³

(d)

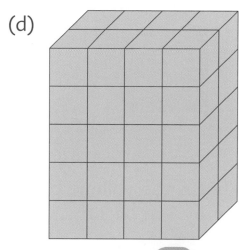

Length = ⬜ cm

Width = ⬜ cm

Height = ⬜ cm

Volume = ⬜ cm³

2. The rectangular prism measures 8 in. by 2 in. by 5 in. Find its volume.

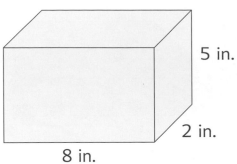

5 in.

2 in.

8 in.

How many 1-in. cubes are needed to build this rectangular prism?

$8 \times 2 \times 5 =$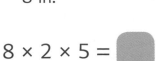

The volume of the rectangular prism is ⬜ in.³.

3. The figure shows a cube of edge 1 m.
The volume of the cube is 1 **cubic meter (m³)**.

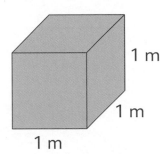

1 m

1 m

1 m

The cubic meter is also a unit of volume. We write **m³** for cubic meter.

What is the volume of a rectangular prism which measures 2 m by 1 m by 1 m?

$2 \times 1 \times 1 =$

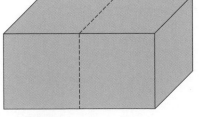

The volume of the rectangular prism is ⬜ m³.

4. Find the volume of a rectangular prism which measures 5 m by 3 m by 4 m.

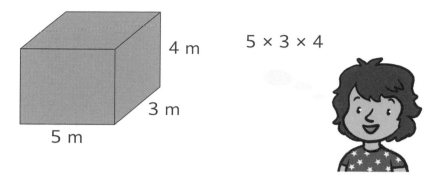

$5 \times 3 \times 4$

5. Find the volume of a cube of edge 3 m.

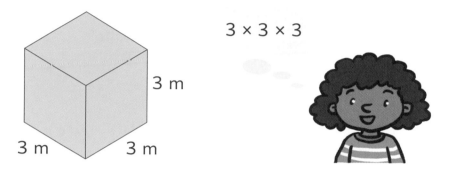

$3 \times 3 \times 3$

6. Find the volume of each of the following rectangular prisms.

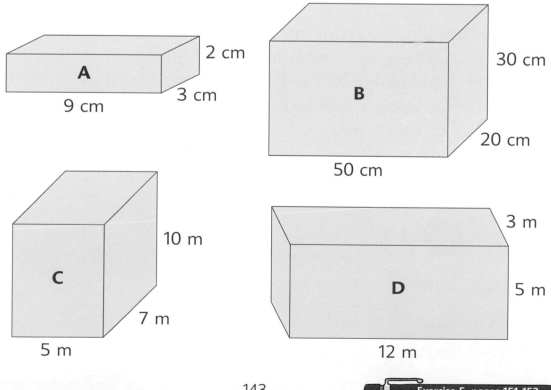

Exercise 5, pages 151-152

7. The rectangular box measures 10 cm by 10 cm by 10 cm.
   It can hold 1 liter of water.

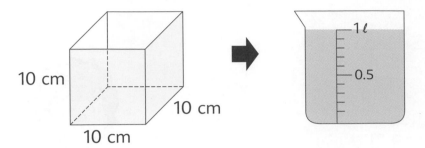

10 cm

10 cm

10 cm

Volume of water in the box = 10 × 10 × 10

=  cm³

1 ℓ =  cm³

1 ℓ = 1000 ml

1 ml = ⬤ cm³

8. Write in cubic centimeters.
   (a) 2 ℓ   (b) 400 ml   (c) 1 ℓ 200 ml

9. Write in liters and milliliters.
   (a) 1750 cm³   (b) 2450 cm³   (c) 3050 cm³

10. A rectangular fish tank measures 30 cm by 20 cm by 20 cm.
    (a) Find its capacity in cubic centimeters.
    (b) If the tank is filled with water to a depth of 8 cm, find
        the volume of the water in liters and milliliters.
        (1 ℓ = 1000 cm³)

    (a) Capacity of the tank
        = 30 × 20 × 20

        = ⬤ cm³

    (b) Volume of water
        = 30 × 20 × 8

        = ⬤ cm³

        = ⬤ ℓ ⬤ ml

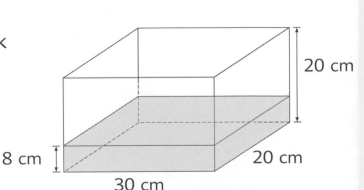

8 cm

30 cm

20 cm

20 cm

144

Exercise 6, pages 153-154

1. The following solids are made up of 1-in. cubes.
   Find the volume of each solid.

   (a) 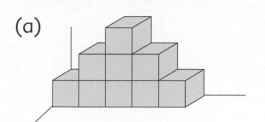   (b)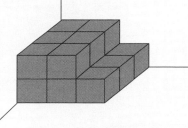

2. A rectangular prism measures
   30 cm by 25 cm by 15 cm.
   Find its volume.

   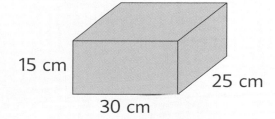

3. Find the volume of a cube of edge 5 cm.

   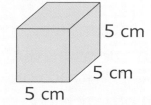

4. A rectangular tank is 12 ft long,
   10 ft wide, and 3 ft high.
   Find its capacity in cubic feet.

   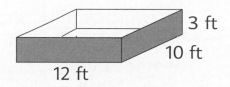

5. How many 1-cm cubes are needed
   to build a cuboid measuring
   8 cm by 5 cm by 3 cm?

   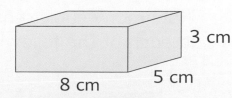

6. A rectangular box measures
   30 cm by 20 cm by 20 cm.
   It is completely filled with sand.
   How many cubic centimeters
   of sand are there in the box?

   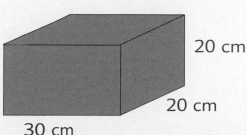

PRACTICE C

1. Write in cubic centimeters.

   (a) 3 ℓ   (b) 250 ml   (c) 2 ℓ 60 ml

2. Write in liters and milliliters.

   (a) 1050 cm³   (b) 1800 cm³   (c) 3500 cm³

3. A rectangular tin measures 15 cm by 10 cm by 3 cm.
   How many milliliters of water can it hold?
   (1 ml = 1 cm³)

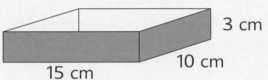

4. A rectangular tank 20 cm long,
   18 cm wide, and 20 cm high is
   filled with colored water to a
   depth of 8 cm.
   (a) Find the volume of water
       in cubic centimeters.
   (b) Express the volume of
       water in liters and milliliters.
       (1 ℓ = 1000 cm³)

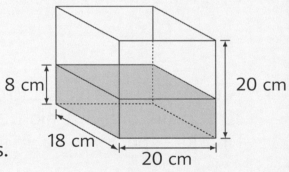

5. How many cubic centimeters of water are there
   in each of the following containers?

   (a)

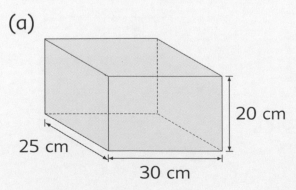

   (b)

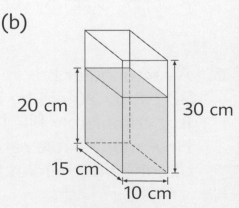

REVIEW 11

1. Arrange the numbers in increasing order.

    (a) 80,431, 79,431, 80,331, 79,433

    (b) 0.6, 0.55, 0.7, 0.09

    (c) $2\frac{2}{9}$, $\frac{9}{2}$, $2\frac{2}{3}$, $2\frac{4}{9}$

    (d) 0, 1, 2, −3, −4, −5

2. Find the value of each of the following. Give the answer in its simplest form.

    (a) $\frac{5}{8} + \frac{5}{8}$ (b) $\frac{2}{3} + \frac{5}{9}$ (c) $5 - \frac{3}{10}$

    (d) $\frac{5}{6} - \frac{2}{3}$ (e) $\frac{2}{7}$ of 28 (f) $\frac{5}{6}$ of 72

3. The figure shows a rectangular field which measures 25 m by 20 m. There is a rectangular flower bed at the center of the field. Find the area of the flower bed.

    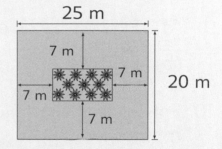

4. (a) How many millimeters must be added to 660 ml to make 1 liter?

    (b) How many grams must be added to 256 g to make 1 kg?

    (c) How many inches must be added to 7 in. to make 1 ft?

    (d) Peter drinks 125 ml of milk a day. How much milk does he drink in two weeks? Give your answer in liters and milliliters.

5. Find the value of each of the following.

    (a) 2 km 740 m + 3 km 590 m   (b) 16 lb − 3 lb 10 oz
    (c) 1 h 25 min + 2 h 45 min   (d) 40 ft 5 in. − 6 ft 10 in.
    (e) 3 ℓ 450 ml × 3   (f) 3 yd 2 ft × 12
    (g) 2 h 45 min × 3   (h) 3 h 20 min ÷ 2

6. Rebecca bought a bag of potatoes that weighed 600 g. She used $\frac{3}{5}$ of the potatoes. How many grams of potatoes did she use?

7. How many 1-in. cubes are needed to build a rectangular prism which measures 6 in. by 2 in. by 3 in.?

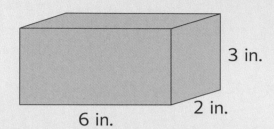

3 in.

2 in.

6 in.

8. (a) $\frac{2}{3}$ of a sum of money is $18. Find the sum of money.

   (b) What is $\frac{1}{4}$ of 32?

9. (a) Express $1\frac{3}{5}$ as a decimal.

   (b) Express 2.05 as a fraction in its simplest form.

10. For each of the following, estimate the product. Then multiply.

   (a) 5637 × 4   (b) 66 × 582   (c) 295 × 49

11. Write **>**, **<**, or **=** in place of each ⬤.

   (a) 306,000 ⬤ 3,006,000

   (b) 80 ⬤ 8000 ÷ 10

   (c) $\frac{2}{5} + \frac{3}{10}$ ⬤ $\frac{2}{3} + \frac{1}{9}$

   (d) $\frac{21}{6}$ ⬤ $2\frac{1}{6}$

   (e) 2 m 90 cm ⬤ 3 m

   (f) 4 gal 2 qt ⬤ 12 pt

12. What is the value of *n* in each of the following?

(a) $7009 - n = 1243$ (b) $4 \times n = 332$

(c) $n \times 4 = 980$ (d) $n \div 7 = 217$

(e) $2.04 = 2 + \dfrac{4}{n}$ (f) $0.45 = 5 \times n$

(g) $(4 + 3) \times n = 70$ (h) $130 + n = 132 + 140$

(i) $36 \times 25 = 9 \times n$ (j) $0.8 = \dfrac{n}{5}$

(k) $5 \div 9 = \dfrac{n}{9}$ (l) $4\dfrac{2}{3} = 3\dfrac{n}{3}$

13. How many faces does the solid have?

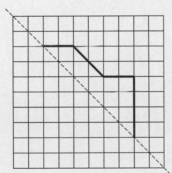

14. Copy and complete the symmetric figure. (The dotted line is a line of symmetry.)

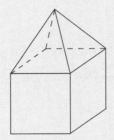

15. Copy and draw a line of symmetry of the symmetric figure.

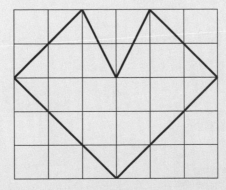

16. Copy and complete the symmetric figure.
(The dotted line is a line of symmetry.)

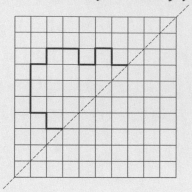

17. Which one of the following is a pair of parallel lines?

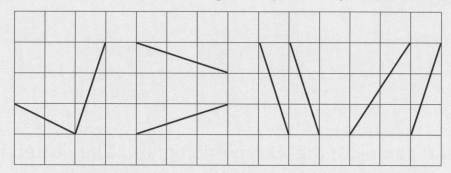

18. Find the perimeter and area of each figure. (All lines meet at right angles.)

(a)

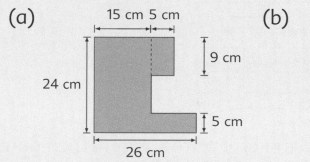

15 cm 5 cm
9 cm
24 cm
5 cm
26 cm

(b)

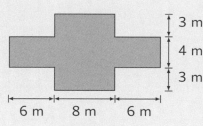

3 m
4 m
3 m
6 m   8 m   6 m

19. Find the area of the shaded part of each rectangle. (All lines meet at right angles.)

(a)

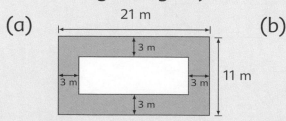

21 m
3 m
3 m   3 m
11 m
3 m

(b)

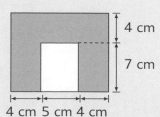

4 cm
7 cm
4 cm 5 cm 4 cm

20. Find the length and perimeter of the rectangle.

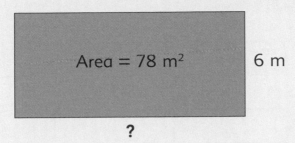

Area = 78 m²   6 m

?

21. The perimeter of a square is 48 in. Find its area.

22. Mrs. Brown used 4.5 m of lace for 5 pillow cases. If she used an equal length of lace for each pillow case, how much lace did she use for each pillow case?

23. Diana saved $70.50 in 5 weeks. If she saved an equal amount each week, how much would she save in 8 weeks?

24. Twice as many concert tickets were sold on Tuesday as on Monday. 40 more tickets were sold on Wednesday than on Tuesday. If 200 tickets were sold on Wednesday, how many tickets were sold on Monday?

25. Chris can choose one type of meat and one type of bread for his sandwich. These are his choices:

MEATS	BREAD
Ham	Rye
Turkey	White
Beef	Sourdough
Pastrami	

How many types of sandwiches can he choose?

26. Mary tossed a number cube labeled 1 to 6 and got the following results.

Results	Number of tosses
1	/
2	//
3	///
4	/
5	//
6	/

(a) What fraction of the tosses gave a result of 3?
(b) What fraction of the tosses gave a result of 5?

27. This graph shows Abe's and Luigi's savings in five months.

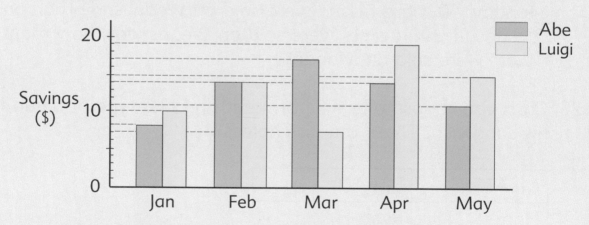

(a) How much did each boy save in January?
(b) In which month did Abe save the most?
(c) In which month did Luigi save the least?
(d) Which boy saved more money in five months?
     How much more?

Review 11, pages 155-163

Grade Four Mathematics Content Standards

By the end of grade four, students understand large numbers and addition, subtraction, multiplication, and division of whole numbers. They describe and compare simple fractions and decimals. They understand the properties of, and the relationships between, plane geometric figures. They collect, represent, and analyze data to answer questions.

Number Sense

1.0   Students understand the place value of whole numbers and decimals to two decimal places and how whole numbers and decimals relate to simple fractions. Students use the concepts of negative numbers:

1.1   Read and write whole numbers in the millions.

1.2   Order and compare whole numbers and decimals to two decimal places.

1.3   Round whole numbers through the millions to the nearest ten, hundred, thousand, ten thousand, or hundred thousand.

1.4   Decide when a rounded solution is called for and explain why such a solution may be appropriate.

1.5   Explain different interpretations of fractions, for example, parts of a whole, parts of a set, and division of whole numbers by whole numbers; explain equivalence of fractions (see Standard 4.0).

1.6   Write tenths and hundredths in decimal and fraction notations and know the fraction and decimal equivalents for halves and fourths (e.g., ½ = 0.5 or 0.50; 7/4 = 1¾ = 1.75).

1.7   Write the fraction represented by a drawing of parts of a figure; represent a given fraction by using drawings; and relate a fraction to a simple decimal on a number line.

1.8   Use concepts of negative numbers (e.g., on a number line, in counting, in temperature, in "owing").

1.9   Identify on a number line the relative position of positive fractions, positive mixed numbers, and positive decimals to two decimal places.

2.0   Students extend their use and understanding of whole numbers to the addition and subtraction of simple decimals:

2.1   Estimate and compute the sum or difference of whole numbers and positive decimals to two places.

2.2   Round two-place decimals to one decimal or to the nearest whole number and judge the reasonableness of the rounded answer.

3.0   Students solve problems involving addition, subtraction, multiplication, and division of whole numbers and understand the relationships among the operations:

3.1   Demonstrate an understanding of, and the ability to use, standard algorithms for the addition and subtraction of multidigit numbers.

3.2   Demonstrate an understanding of, and the ability to use, standard algorithms for multiplying a multidigit number by a two-digit number and for dividing a multidigit number by a one-digit number; use relationships between them to simplify computations and to check results.

3.3   Solve problems involving multiplication of multidigit numbers by two-digit numbers.

3.4   Solve problems involving division of multidigit numbers by one-digit numbers.

4.0   Students know how to factor small whole numbers:

4.1   Understand that many whole numbers break down in different ways (e.g., $12 = 4 \times 3 = 2 \times 6 = 2 \times 2 \times 3$).

4.2   Know that numbers such as 2, 3, 5, 7, and 11 do not have any factors except 1 and themselves and that such numbers are called prime numbers.

Algebra and Functions

1.0   Students use and interpret variables, mathematical symbols, and properties to write and simplify expressions and sentences:

1.1   Use letters, boxes, or other symbols to stand for any number in simple expressions or equations (e.g., demonstrate an understanding and the use of the concept of a variable).

1.2   Interpret and evaluate mathematical expressions that now use parentheses.

1.3   Use parentheses to indicate which operation to perform first when writing expressions containing more than two terms and different operations.

1.4   Use and interpret formulas (e.g., area = length $\times$ width or $A = lw$) to answer questions about quantities and their relationships.

1.5   Understand that an equation such as $y = 3x + 5$ is a prescription for determining a second number when a first number is given.

2.0   Students know how to manipulate equations:

2.1   Know and understand that equals added to equals are equal.

2.2   Know and understand that equals multiplied by equals are equal.

Measurement and Geometry

1.0   Students understand perimeter and area:

1.1   Measure the area of rectangular shapes by using appropriate units, such as square centimeter (cm^2), square meter (m^2), square kilometer (km^2), square inch (in.^{2}), square yard (yd.^{2}), or square mile (mi.^{2}).

1.2   Recognize that rectangles that have the same area can have different perimeters.

1.3   Understand that rectangles that have the same perimeter can have different areas.

1.4   Understand and use formulas to solve problems involving perimeters and areas of rectangles and squares. Use those formulas to find the areas of more complex figures by dividing the figures into basic shapes.

2.0 **Students use two-dimensional coordinate grids to represent points and graph lines and simple figures:**

   2.1   Draw the points corresponding to linear relationships on graph paper (e.g., draw 10 points on the graph of the equation $y = 3x$ and connect them by using a straight line).

   2.2   Understand that the length of a horizontal line segment equals the difference of the x-coordinates.

   2.3   Understand that the length of a vertical line segment equals the difference of the y-coordinates.

3.0 **Students demonstrate an understanding of plane and solid geometric objects and use this knowledge to show relationships and solve problems:**

   3.1   Identify lines that are parallel and perpendicular. (Teachers are advised to introduce the terms intersecting lines and nonintersecting lines when dealing with this standard.)

   3.2   Identify the radius and diameter of a circle.

   3.3   Identify congruent figures.

   3.4   Identify figures that have bilateral and rotational symmetry.

   3.5   Know the definitions of a right angle, an acute angle, and an obtuse angle. Understand that 90°, 180°, 270°, and 360° are associated, respectively, with ¼, ½, ¾ and full turns.

   3.6   Visualize, describe, and make models of geometric solids (e.g., prisms, pyramids) in terms of the number and shape of faces, edges, and vertices; interpret two-dimensional representations of three-dimensional objects; and draw patterns (of faces) for a solid that, when cut and folded, will make a model of the solid.

   3.7   Know the definitions of different triangles (e.g., equilateral, isosceles, scalene) and identify their attributes.

   3.8   Know the definition of different quadrilaterals (e.g., rhombus, square, rectangle, parallelogram, trapezoid).

Statistics, Data Analysis, and Probability

1.0 **Students organize, represent, and interpret numerical and categorical data and clearly communicate their findings:**

   1.1   Formulate survey questions; systematically collect and represent data on a number line; and coordinate graphs, tables, and charts.

   1.2   Identify the mode(s) for sets of categorical data and the mode(s), median, and any apparent outliers for numerical data sets.

   1.3   Interpret one- and two-variable data graphs to answer questions about a situation.

2.0   Students make predictions for simple probability situations:

    2.1   Represent all possible outcomes for a simple probability situation in an organized way (e.g., tables, grids, tree diagrams).

    2.2   Express outcomes of experimental probability situations verbally and numerically (e.g., 3 out of 4; ¾).

Mathematical Reasoning

1.0   Students make decisions about how to approach problems:

    1.1   Analyze problems by identifying relationships, distinguishing relevant from irrelevant information, sequencing and prioritizing information, and observing patterns.

    1.2   Determine when and how to break a problem into simpler parts.

2.0   Students use strategies, skills, and concepts in finding solutions:

    2.1   Use estimation to verify the reasonableness of calculated results.

    2.2   Apply strategies and results from simpler problems to more complex problems.

    2.3   Use a variety of methods, such as words, numbers, symbols, charts, graphs, tables, diagrams, and models, to explain mathematical reasoning.

    2.4   Express the solution clearly and logically by using the appropriate mathematical notation and terms and clear language; support solutions with evidence in both verbal and symbolic work.

    2.5   Indicate the relative advantages of exact and approximate solutions to problems and give answers to a specified degree of accuracy.

    2.6   Make precise calculations and check the validity of the results from the context of the problem.

3.0   Students move beyond a particular problem by generalizing to other situations:

    3.1   Evaluate the reasonableness of the solution in the context of the original situation.

    3.2   Note the method of deriving the solution and demonstrate a conceptual understanding of the derivation by solving similar problems.

    3.3   Develop generalizations of the results obtained and apply them in other circumstances.

GLOSSARY

Word	Meaning
congruent figures	When two shapes have the same size and shape, they are called **congruent figures**.
coordinates	The numbers in an ordered pair are called **coordinates**. They tell us how to locate something on a grid. 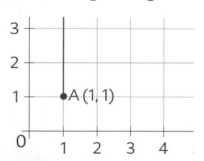 Point A is located at (1, 1).
decimal	A **decimal** is a number that shows the place values that are less than one such as tenths, hundredths or thousandths.

Ones	Tenths	Hundredths	Thousandths
3	1	8	2

3.182 is a decimal.

Word	Meaning
decimal places	The tenths place, hundredths place and thousandths place are called **decimal places**.
decimal point	The dot '.' in a decimal is called a **decimal point**.
line of symmetry	A **line of symmetry** divides a figure into two halves that fit exactly.
line symmetry	A figure has **line symmetry** when one half of it folds into the other half.
median	The middle number of a set of data is called the **median**.
mode	The value that appears most often in a set of data is called the **mode**.

Word	Meaning
ordered pair	In an **ordered pair**, the first number tells us how far to move horizontally and the second number tells us how far to move vertically to locate an object.
rotational symmetry	A figure has **rotational symmetry** if it can be turned around a central point and still look the same in at least one position other than the starting one.
tessellation	A **tessellation** is a tiling pattern made up of congruent shapes.
volume	The **volume** of a solid is the amount of space it occupies. Volume of a rectangular prism = length × width × height

Index